AWS Certified Cloud Practitioner Practice Tests 20

400 AWS Practice with Answers

G000067288

~

Nicola Erbacci

1. Under the shared responsibility model, which of the following is the customer responsible for?

    A. Ensuring that disk drives are wiped after use.
    B. Ensuring that rmware is updated on hardware devices.
    C. Ensuring that data is encrypted at rest.
    D. Ensuring that network cables are category six or higher.

2. The use of what AWS feature or service allows companies to track and categorize spending on a detailed level?

    A. Cost allocation tags
    B. Consolidated billing
    C. AWS Budgets
    D. AWS Marketplace

3. Which service stores objects, provides real-time access to those objects, and offers versioning and lifecycle capabilities?

    A. Amazon Glacier
    B. AWS Storage Gateway
    C. Amazon S3
    D. Amazon EBS

4. What AWS team assists customers with accelerating cloud adoption through paid engagements in any of several specialty practice areas?

    A. AWS Enterprise Support
    B. AWS Solutions Architects
    C. AWS Professional Services
    D. AWS Account Managers

5. A customer would like to design and build a new workload on AWS Cloud but does not have the AWS-related software technical expertise inhouse. Which of the following AWS programs can a customer take advantage of to achieve that outcome?

    A. AWS Partner Network Technology Partners
    B. AWS Marketplace
    C. AWS Partner Network Consulting Partners
    D. AWS Service Catalog

6. Distributing workloads across multiple Availability Zones supports which cloud architecture design principle?

    A. Implement automation.
    B. Design for agility.
    C. Design for failure
    D. Implement elasticity.

7. Which AWS services can host a Microsoft SQL Server database? (Choose two.)

    A. Amazon EC2
    B. Amazon Relational Database Service (Amazon RDS)
    C. Amazon Aurora
    D. Amazon Redshift
    E. Amazon S3

8. Which of the following inspects AWS environments to nd opportunities that can save money for users and also improve system performance?

    A. AWS Cost Explorer
    B. AWS Trusted Advisor
    C. Consolidated billing
    D. Detailed billing

9. Which of the following Amazon EC2 pricing models allow customers to use existing server-bound software licenses?

    A. Spot Instances

    B. Reserved Instances

    ✓ C. Dedicated Hosts

    (D.) On-Demand Instances

10. Which AWS characteristics make AWS cost effective for a workload with dynamic user demand? (Choose two.)

    A. High availability

    B. Shared security model

    ✓ (C.) Elasticity

    ✓ (D.) Pay-as-you-go pricing

    E. Reliability

11. Which service enables risk auditing by continuously monitoring and logging account activity, including user actions in the AWS Management Console and AWS SDKs?

    A. Amazon CloudWatch

    ✓ B. AWS CloudTrail

    C. AWS Config

    (D.) AWS Health

12. Which of the following are characteristics of Amazon S3? (Choose two.)

    A. A global file system

    ✓ (B.) An object store

    C. A local file store

    (D.) A network file system

    ✓ E. A durable storage

13. Which services can be used across hybrid AWS Cloud architectures? (Choose two.)

   A. Amazon Route 53
   B. Virtual Private Gateway
   C. Classic Load Balancer
   D. Auto Scaling
   E. Amazon CloudWatch default metrics

14. What costs are included when comparing AWS Total Cost of Ownership (TCO) with on-premises TCO?

   A. Project management
   B. Antivirus software licensing
   C. Data center security
   D. Software development

15. A company is considering using AWS for a self-hosted database that requires a nightly shutdown for maintenance and cost-saving purposes. Which service should the company use?

   A. Amazon Redshift
   B. Amazon DynamoDB
   C. Amazon Elastic Compute Cloud (Amazon EC2) with Amazon EC2 instance store
   D. Amazon EC2 with Amazon Elastic Block Store (Amazon EBS)

16. Which of the following is a correct relationship between regions, Availability Zones, and edge locations?

   A. Data centers contain regions.
   B. Regions contain Availability Zones.
   C. Availability Zones contain edge locations.
   D. Edge locations contain regions.

17. Which AWS tools assist with estimating costs? (Choose three.)

   A. Detailed billing report
   B. Cost allocation tags
   C. AWS Simple Monthly Calculator
   D. AWS Total Cost of Ownership (TCO) Calculator
   E. Cost Estimator

18. Which of the following are advantages of AWS consolidated billing? (Choose two.)

   A. The ability to receive one bill for multiple accounts
   B. Service limits increasing by default in all accounts
   C. A fixed discount on the monthly bill
   D. Potential volume discounts, as usage in all accounts is combined
   E. The automatic extension of the master account›s AWS support plan to all accounts

19. Which of the following Reserved Instance (RI) pricing models provides the highest average savings compared to On-Demand pricing?

   A. One-year, No Upfront, Standard RI pricing
   B. One-year, All Upfront, Convertible RI pricing
   C. Three-year, All Upfront, Standard RI pricing
   D. Three-year, No Upfront, Convertible RI pricing

20. Compared with costs in traditional and virtualized data centers, AWS has:

   A. greater variable costs and greater upfront costs.
   B. fixed usage costs and lower upfront costs.
   C. lower variable costs and greater upfront costs.
   D. lower variable costs and lower upfront costs.

5

21. A characteristic of edge locations is that they:

    A. host Amazon EC2 instances closer to users.
    B. help lower latency and improve performance for users.
    C. cache frequently changing data without reaching the origin server.
    D. refresh data changes daily.

22. Which of the following can limit Amazon Storage Service (Amazon S3) bucket access to specic users?

    A. A public and private key-pair
    B. Amazon Inspector
    C. AWS Identity and Access Management (IAM) policies
    D. Security Groups

23. Which of the following security-related actions are available at no cost?

    A. Calling AWS Support
    B. Contacting AWS Professional Services to request a workshop
    C. Accessing forums, blogs, and whitepapers
    D. Attending AWS classes at a local university

24. Which of the Reserved Instance (RI) pricing models can change the attributes of the RI as long as the exchange results in the creation of RIs of equal or greater value?

    A. Dedicated RIs
    B. Scheduled RIs
    C. Convertible RIs
    D. Standard RIs

25. Which AWS feature will reduce the customer's total cost of ownership (TCO)?

    A. Shared responsibility security model

    B. Single tenancy

    C. Elastic computing

    D. Encryption

26. Which of the following services will automatically scale with an expected increase in web traffic?

    A. AWS CodePipeline

    B. Elastic Load Balancing

    C. Amazon EBS

    D. AWS Direct Connect

27. Where are AWS compliance documents, such as an SOC 1 report, located?

    A. Amazon Inspector

    B. AWS CloudTrail

    C. AWS Artifact

    D. AWS Certificate Manager

28. Under the AWS shared responsibility model, which of the following activities are the customer's responsibility? (Choose two.)

    A. Patching operating system components for Amazon Relational Database Server (Amazon RDS)

    B. Encrypting data on the client-side

    C. Training the data center staff

    D. Configuring Network Access Control Lists (ACL)

    E. Maintaining environmental controls within a data center

29. Which is a recommended pattern for designing a highly available architecture on AWS?

    A. Ensure that components have low-latency network connectivity.

    B. Run enough Amazon EC2 instances to operate at peak load.

    C. Ensure that the application is designed to accommodate failure of any single component.

    D. Use a monolithic application that handles all operations.

30. According to best practices, how should an application be designed to run in the AWS Cloud?

    A. Use tightly coupled components.

    B. Use loosely coupled components.

    C. Use infrequently coupled components.

    D. Use frequently coupled components.

31. AWS supports which of the following methods to add security to Identity and Access Management (IAM) users? (Choose two.)

    A. Implementing Amazon Rekognition

    B. Using AWS Shield-protected resources

    C. Blocking access with Security Groups

    D. Using Multi-Factor Authentication (MFA)

    E. Enforcing password strength and expiration

32. Which AWS services should be used for read/write of constantly changing data? (Choose two.)

A. Amazon Glacier
B. Amazon RDS
C. AWS Snowball
D. Amazon Redshift
E. Amazon EFS

33. What is one of the advantages of the Amazon Relational Database Service (Amazon RDS)?

A. It simplifies relational database administration tasks.
B. It provides 99.99999999999% reliability and durability.
C. It automatically scales databases for loads.
D. It enables users to dynamically adjust CPU and RAM resources.

34. A customer needs to run a MySQL database that easily scales. Which AWS service should they use?

A. Amazon Aurora
B. Amazon Redshift
C. Amazon DynamoDB
D. Amazon ElastiCache

35. Which of the following components of the AWS Global Infrastructure consists of one or more discrete data centers interconnected through low latency links?

A. Availability Zone
B. Edge location
C. Region
D. Private networking

36. Which of the following is a shared control between the customer and AWS?

    A. Providing a key for Amazon S3 client-side encryption
    B. Configuration of an Amazon EC2 instance
    C. Environmental controls of physical AWS data centers
    D. Awareness and training

37. How many Availability Zones should compute resources be provisioned across to achieve high availability?

    A. A minimum of one
    B. A minimum of two
    C. A minimum of three
    D. A minimum of four or more

38. One of the advantages to moving infrastructure from an on-premises data center to the AWS Cloud is:

    A. it allows the business to eliminate IT bills.
    B. it allows the business to put a server in each customer's data center.
    C. it allows the business to focus on business activities.
    D. it allows the business to leave servers unpatched.

39. What is the lowest-cost, durable storage option for retaining database backups for immediate retrieval?

    A. Amazon S3
    B. Amazon Glacier
    C. Amazon EBS
    D. Amazon EC2 Instance Store

40. Which AWS IAM feature allows developers to access AWS services through the AWS CLI?

    A. API keys
    B. Access keys
    C. User names/Passwords
    D. SSH keys

41. Which of the following is a fast and reliable NoSQL database service?

    A. Amazon Redshift
    B. Amazon RDS
    C. Amazon DynamoDB
    D. Amazon S3

42. What is an example of agility in the AWS Cloud?

    A. Access to multiple instance types
    B. Access to managed services
    C. Using Consolidated Billing to produce one bill
    D. Decreased acquisition time for new compute resources

43. Which service should a customer use to consolidate and centrally manage multiple AWS accounts?

    A. AWS IAM
    B. AWS Organizations
    C. AWS Schema Conversion Tool
    D. AWS Config

44. What approach to transcoding a large number of individual video files adheres to AWS architecture principles?

A. Using many instances in parallel

B. Using a single large instance during off-peak hours

C. Using dedicated hardware

D. Using a large GPU instance type

45. For which auditing process does AWS have sole responsibility?

A. AWS IAM policies

B. Physical security

C. Amazon S3 bucket policies

D. AWS CloudTrail Logs

46. Which feature of the AWS Cloud will support an international company's requirement for low latency to all of its customers?

A. Fault tolerance

B. Global reach

C. Pay-as-you-go pricing

D. High availability

47. Which of the following is the customer's responsibility under the AWS shared responsibility model?

A. Patching underlying infrastructure

B. Physical security

C. Patching Amazon EC2 instances

D. Patching network infrastructure

48. A customer is using multiple AWS accounts with separate billing. How can the customer take advantage of volume discounts with minimal impact to the AWS resources?

    A. Create one global AWS acount and move all AWS resources to tha account.

    B. Sign up for three years of Reserved Instance pricing up front.

    C. Use the consolidated billing feature from AWS Organizations.

    D. Sign up for the AWS Enterprise support plan to get volume discounts.

49. Which of the following are features of Amazon CloudWatch Logs? (Choose two.)

    A. Summaries by Amazon Simple Notification Service (Amazon SNS)

    B. Free Amazon Elasticsearch Service analytics

    C. Provided at no charge

    D. Real-time monitoring

    E. Adjustable retention

50. Which of the following is an AWS managed Domain Name System (DNS) web service?

    A. Amazon Route 53

    B. Amazon Neptune

    C. Amazon SageMaker

    D. Amazon Lightsail

51. A customer is deploying a new application and needs to choose an AWS Region. Which of the following factors could influence the customer's decision? (Select TWO.)

    A. Reduced latency to users
    B. The application's presentation in the local language
    C. Data sovereignty compliance
    D. Cooling costs in hotter climates
    E. Proximity to the customer's ofice for on-site visits

52. Which storage service can be used as a low-cost option for hosting static websites?

    A. Amazon Glacier
    B. Amazon DynamoDB
    C. Amazon Elastic File System (Amazon EFS)
    D. Amazon Simple Storage Service (Amazon S3)

53. Which Amazon EC2 instance pricing model can provide discounts of up to 90%?

    A. Reserved Instances
    B. On-Demand
    C. Dedicated Hosts
    D. Spot Instances

54. What is the AWS customer responsible for according to the AWS shared responsibility model?

    A. Physical access controls
    B. Data encryption
    C. Secure disposal of storage devices
    D. Environmental risk management

55. Which of the following AWS Cloud services can be used to run a customer-managed relational database?

    A. Amazon EC2
    B. Amazon Route 53
    C. Amazon ElastiCache
    D. Amazon DynamoDB

56. A company is looking for a scalable data warehouse solution. Which of the following AWS solutions would meet the company's needs?

    A. Amazon Simple Storage Service (Amazon S3)
    B. Amazon DynamoDB
    C. Amazon Kinesis
    D. Amazon Redshift

57. Which statement best describes Elastic Load Balancing?

    A. It translates a domain name into an IP address using DNS.
    B. It distributes incoming application trafic across one or more Amazon EC2 instances.
    C. It collects metrics on connected Amazon EC2 instances.
    D. It automatically adjusts the number of Amazon EC2 instances to support incoming trafic.

58. Which of the following are valid ways for a customer to interact with AWS services? (Choose two.)

    A. Command line interface
    B. On-premises
    C. Software Development Kits
    D. Software-as-a-service
    E. Hybrid

59. The AWS Cloud's multiple Regions are an example of:

   A. agility.
   B. global infrastructure.
   C. elasticity.
   D. pay-as-you-go pricing.

60. Which of the following AWS services can be used to serve large amounts of online video content with the lowest possible latency? (Choose two.)

   A. AWS Storage Gateway
   B. Amazon S3
   C. Amazon Elastic File System (EFS)
   D. Amazon Glacier
   E. Amazom CloudFront

61. Web servers running on Amazon EC2 access a legacy application running in a corporate data center. What term would describe this model?

   A. Cloud-native
   B. Partner network
   C. Hybrid architecture
   D. Infrastructure as a service

62. What is the benefit of using AWS managed services, such as Amazon ElastiCache and Amazon Relational Database Service (Amazon RDS)?

   A. They require the customer to monitor and replace failing instances.
   B. They have better performance than customer-managed services.
   C. They simplify patching and updating underlying OSs.
   D. They do not require the customer to optimize instance type or size selections.

63. Which service provides a virtually unlimited amount of online highly durable object storage?

   A. Amazon Redshift
   B. Amazon Elastic File System (Amazon EFS)
   C. Amazon Elastic Container Service (Amazon ECS)
   D. Amazon S3

64. Which of the following Identity and Access Management (IAM) entities is associated with an access key ID and secret access key when using AWS Command Line Interface (AWS CLI)?

   A. IAM group
   B. IAM user
   C. IAM role
   D. IAM policy

65. Which of the following security-related services does AWS offer? (Choose two.)

   A. Multi-factor authentication physical tokens
   B. AWS Trusted Advisor security checks
   C. Data encryption
   D. Automated penetration testing
   E. Amazon S3 copyrighted content detection

66. Which AWS managed service is used to host databases?

   A. AWS Batch
   B. AWS Artifact
   C. AWS Data Pipeline
   D. Amazon RDS

67. Which AWS service provides a simple and scalable shared file storage solution for use with Linux-based AWS and on-premises servers?

   A. Amazon S3
   B. Amazon Glacier
   C. Amazon Elastic Block Store (Amazon EBS)
   D. Amazon Elastic File System (Amazon EFS)

68. When architecting cloud applications, which of the following are a key design principle?

   A. Use the largest instance possible
   B. Provision capacity for peak load
   C. Use the Scrum development process
   D. Implement elasticity

69. Which AWS service should be used for long-term, low-cost storage of data backups?

A. Amazon RDS

B. Amazon Glacier

C. AWS Snowball

D. AWS EBS

70. Under the shared responsibility model, which of the following is a shared control between a customer and AWS?

A. Physical controls

B. Patch management

C. Zone security

D. Data center auditing

71. Which AWS service allows companies to connect an Amazon VPC to an on-premises data center?

A. AWS VPN

B. Amazon Redshift

C. API Gateway

D. Amazon Connect

72. A company wants to reduce the physical compute footprint that developers use to run code. Which service would meet that need by enabling serverless architectures?

A. Amazon Elastic Compute Cloud (Amazon EC2)

B. AWS Lambda

C. Amazon DynamoDB

D. AWS CodeCommit

73. Which AWS service provides alerts when an AWS event may impact a company's AWS resources?

   A. AWS Personal Health Dashboard
   B. AWS Service Health Dashboard
   C. AWS Trusted Advisor
   D. AWS Infrastructure Event Management

74. Which of the following are categories of AWS Trusted Advisor? (Choose two.)

   A. Fault Tolerance
   B. Instance Usage
   C. Infrastructure
   D. Performance
   E. Storage Capacity

75. Which task is AWS responsible for in the shared responsibility model for security and compliance?

   A. Granting access to individuals and services
   B. Encrypting data in transit
   C. Updating Amazon EC2 host firmware
   D. Updating operating systems

76. Where should a company go to search software listings from independent software vendors to find, test, buy and deploy software that runs on AWS?

   A. AWS Marketplace
   B. Amazon Lumberyard
   C. AWS Artifact
   D. Amazon CloudSearch

77. Which of the following is a benefit of using the AWS Cloud?

   A. Permissive security removes the administrative burden.
   B. Ability to focus on revenue-generating activities.
   C. Control over cloud network hardware.
   D. Choice of specific cloud hardware vendors.

78. When performing a cost analysis that supports physical isolation of a customer workload, which compute hosting model should be accounted for in the Total Cost of Ownership (TCO)?

   A. Dedicated Hosts
   B. Reserved Instances
   C. On-Demand Instances
   D. No Upfront Reserved Instances

79. Which AWS service provides the ability to manage infrastructure as code?

   A. AWS CodePipeline
   B. AWS CodeDeploy
   C. AWS Direct Connect
   D. AWS CloudFormation

80. If a customer needs to audit the change management of AWS resources, which of the following AWS services should the customer use?

   A. AWS Config
   B. AWS Trusted Advisor
   C. Amazon CloudWatch
   D. Amazon Inspector

81. What is Amazon CloudWatch?

   A. A code repository with customizable build and team commit features.

   B. A metrics repository with customizable notification thresholds and channels.

   C. A security configuration repository with threat analytics.

   D. A rule repository of a web application firewall with automated vulnerability prevention features.

82. Which service allows a company with multiple AWS accounts to combine its usage to obtain volume discounts?

   A. AWS Server Migration Service

   B. AWS Organizations

   C. AWS Budgets

   D. AWS Trusted Advisor

83. Which of the following services could be used to deploy an application to servers running on-premises? (Choose two.)

   A. AWS Elastic Beanstalk

   B. AWS OpsWorks

   C. AWS CodeDeploy

   D. AWS Batch

   E. AWS X-Ray

84. Which Amazon EC2 pricing model adjusts based on supply and demand of EC2 instances?

   A. On-Demand Instances

   B. Reserved Instances

   C. Spot Instances

   D. Convertible Reserved Instances

85. Which design principles for cloud architecture are recommended when re-architecting a large monolithic application? (Choose two.)

   A. Use manual monitoring.

   B. Use fixed servers.

   C. Implement loose coupling.

   D. Rely on individual components.

   E. Design for scalability.

86. Which is the MINIMUM AWS Support plan that allows for one-hour target response time for support cases?

   A. Enterprise

   B. Business

   C. Developer

   D. Basic

87. Where can AWS compliance and certification reports be downloaded?

   A. AWS Artifact

   B. AWS Concierge

   C. AWS Certificate Manager

   D. AWS Trusted Advisor

88. Which AWS service provides a customized view of the health of specific AWS services that power a customer's workloads running on AWS?

   A. AWS Service Health Dashboard

   B. AWS X-Ray

   C. AWS Personal Health Dashboard

   D. Amazon CloudWatch

89. Which of the following is an advantage of consolidated billing on AWS?

    A. Volume pricing qualification

    B. Shared access permissions

    C. Multiple bills per account

    D. Eliminates the need for tagging

90. Which of the following steps should be taken by a customer when conducting penetration testing on AWS?

    A. Conduct penetration testing using Amazon Inspector, and then notify AWS support.

    B. Request and wait for approval from the customer's internal security team, and then conduct testing.

    C. Notify AWS support, and then conduct testing immediately.

    D. Request and wait for approval from AWS support, and then conduct testing.

91. Which of the following AWS features enables a user to launch a pre-configured Amazon Elastic Compute Cloud (Amazon EC2) instance?

    A. Amazon Elastic Block Store (Amazon EBS)

    B. Amazon Machine Image

    C. Amazon EC2 Systems Manager

    D. Amazon AppStream 2.0

92. How would an AWS customer easily apply common access controls to a large set of users?

A. Apply an IAM policy to an IAM group.

B. Apply an IAM policy to an IAM role.

C. Apply the same IAM policy to all IAM users with access to the same workload.

D. Apply an IAM policy to an Amazon Cognito user pool.

93. What technology enables compute capacity to adjust as loads change?

A. Load balancing

B. Automatic Failover

C. Round robin

D. Auto Scaling

94. Which AWS servics are defined as global instead of regional? (Chosee two)

A. Amazon Route 53

B. Amazon EC2

C. Amazon S3

D. Amazon CloudFront

E. Amazon DynamoDB

95. Which AWS service would you use to obtain compliance reports and certificates?

A. AWS Artifact

B. AWS Lambda

C. Amazon Inspector

D. AWS Certificate Manager

96. Under the shared responsibility model, which of the following tasks are the responsibility of the AWS customer? (Choose two.)

   A. Ensuring that application data is encrypted at rest
   B. Ensuring that AWS NTP servers are set to the correct time
   C. Ensuring that users have received security training in the use of AWS services
   D. Ensuring that access to data centers is restricted
   E. Ensuring that hardware is disposed of properly

97. Which AWS service can be used to manually launch instances based on resource requirements?

   A. Amazon EBS
   B. Amazon S3
   C. Amazon EC2
   D. Amazon ECS

98. A company is migrating an application that is running non-interruptible workloads for a three-year time frame. Which pricing construct would provide the MOST cost-effective solution?

   A. Amazon EC2 Spot Instances
   B. Amazon EC2 Dedicated Instances
   C. Amazon EC2 On-Demand Instances
   D. Amazon EC2 Reserved Instances

99. The financial benefits of using AWS are: (Choose two.)

   A. reduced Total Cost of Ownership (TCO).
   B. increased capital expenditure (capex).
   C. reduced operational expenditure (opex).
   D. deferred payment plans for startups.
   E. business credit lines for stratups.

100. Which AWS Cost Management tool allows you to view the most granular data about your AWS bill?

  A. AWS Cost Explorer

  B. AWS Budgets

  C. AWS Cost and Usage report

  D. AWS Billing dashboard

101. Which of the following can an AWS customer use to launch a new Amazon Relational Database Service (Amazon RDS) cluster?

  A. AWS Concierge

  B. AWS CloudFormation

  C. Amazon Simple Storage Service (Amazon S3)

  D. Amazon EC2 Auto Scaling

  E. AWS Management Console

102. Which of the following is an AWS Cloud architecture design principle?

  A. Implement single points of failure.

  B. Implement loose coupling.

  C. Implement monolithic design.

  D. Implement vertical scaling.

103. Which of the following security measures protect access to an AWS account? (Choose two.)

  A. Enable AWS CloudTrail.

  B. Grant least privilege access to IAM users.

  C. Create one IAM user and share with many developers and users.

  D. Enable Amazon CloudFront.

  E. Activate multi-factor authentication (MFA) for privileged users

104. Which service provides a hybrid storage service that enables on-premises applications to seamlessly use cloud storage?

    A. Amazon Glacier
    B. AWS Snowball
    C. AWS Storage Gateway
    D. Amazon Elastic Block Storage (Amazon EBS)

105. Which of the following services falls under the responsibility of the customer to maintain operating system configuration, security patching, and networking?

    A. Amazon RDS
    B. Amazon EC2
    C. Amazon ElastiCache
    D. AWS Fargate

106. Which of the following is an important architectural design principle when designing cloud applications?

    A. Use multiple Availability Zones.
    B. Use tightly coupled components.
    C. Use open source software.
    D. Provision extra capacity.

107. Which AWS support plan includes a dedicated Technical Account Manager?ù

    A. Developer
    B. Enterprise
    C. Business
    D. Basic

108. Amazon Relational Database Service (Amazon RDS) offers which of the following bene

   A. AWS manages the data stored in Amazon RDS tables.
   B. AWS manages the maintenance of the operating system.
   C. AWS automatically scales up instance types on demand.
   D. AWS manages the database type.

109. Which service is best for storing common database query results, which helps to alleviate database access load?

   A. Amazon Machine Learning
   B. Amazon SQS
   C. Amazon ElastiCache
   D. Amazon EC2 Instance Store

110. Which of the following is a component of the shared responsibility model managed entirely by AWS?

   A. Patching operating system software
   B. Encrypting data
   C. Enforcing multi-factor authentication
   D. Auditing physical data center assets

111. Which options does AWS make available for customers who want to learn about security in the cloud in an instructor-led setting? (Choose two.)

   A. AWS Trusted Advisor
   B. AWS Online Tech Talks
   C. AWS Blog
   D. AWS Forums
   E. AWS Classroom Training

112. Which of the following features can be configured through the Amazon Virtual Private Cloud (Amazon VPC) Dashboard? (Choose two.)

    A. Amazon CloudFront distributions

    B. Amazon Route 53

    C. Security Groups

    D. Subnets

    E. Elastic Load Balancing

113. If each department within a company has its own AWS account, what is one way to enable consolidated billing?

    A. Use AWS Budgets on each account to pay only to budget.

    B. Contact AWS Support for a monthly bill.

    C. Create an AWS Organization from the payer account and invite the other accounts to join.

    D. Put all invoices into one Amazon Simple Storage Service (Amazon S3) bucket, load data into Amazon Redshift, and then run a billing report.

114. How do customers benefit from Amazon's massive economies of scale?

    A. Periodic price reductions as the result of Amazon's operational eficiencies

    B. New Amazon EC2 instance types providing the latest hardware

    C. The ability to scale up and down when needed

    D. Increased reliability in the underlying hardware of Amazon EC2 instances

115. Which AWS services can be used to gather information about AWS account activity? (Choose two.)

A. Amazon CloudFront

B. AWS Cloud9

C. AWS CloudTrail

D. AWS CloudHSM

E. Amazon CloudWatch

116. Which of the following common IT tasks can AWS cover to free up company IT resources? (Choose two.)

A. Patching databases software

B. Testing application releases

C. Backing up databases

D. Creating database schema

E. Running penetration tests

117. In which scenario should Amazon EC2 Spot Instances be used?

A. A company wants to move its main website to AWS from an on-premises web server.

B. A company has a number of application services whose Service Level Agreement (SLA) requires 99.999% uptime.

C. A company's heavily used legacy database is currently running on-premises.

D. A company has a number of infrequent, interruptible jobs that are currently using On-Demand Instances.

118. Which AWS feature should a customer leverage to achieve high availability of an application?

   A. AWS Direct Connect
   B. Availability Zones
   C. Data centers
   D. Amazon Virtual Private Cloud (Amazon VPC)

119. Which is the minimum AWS Support plan that includes Infrastructure Event Management without additional costs?

   A. Enterprise
   B. Business
   C. Developer
   D. Basic

120. Which AWS service can serve a static website?

   A. Amazon S3
   B. Amazon Route 53
   C. Amazon QuickSight
   D. AWS X-Ray

121. How does AWS shorten the time to provision IT resources?

   A. It supplies an online IT ticketing platform for resource requests.
   B. It supports automatic code validation services.
   C. It provides the ability to programmatically provision existing resources.
   D. It automates the resource request process from a company's IT vendor list.

122. What can AWS edge locations be used for? (Choose two.)

    A. Hosting applications
    B. Delivering content closer to users
    C. Running NoSQL database caching services
    D. Reducing trafic on the server by caching responses
    E. Sending notification messages to end users

123. Which of the following can limit Amazon Simple Storage Service (Amazon S3) bucket access to specific users?

    A. A public and private key-pair
    B. Amazon Inspector
    C. AWS Identity and Access Management (IAM) policies
    D. Security Groups

124. A solution that is able to support growth in users, trafic, or data size with no drop in performance aligns with which cloud architecture principle?

    A. Think parallel
    B. Implement elasticity
    C. Decouple your components
    D. Design for failure

125. A company will be moving from an on-premises data center to the AWS Cloud.

What would be one financial difference after the move?

A. Moving from variable operational expense (opex) to upfront capital expense (capex).

B. Moving from upfront capital expense (capex) to variable capital expense (capex).

C. Moving from upfront capital expense (capex) to variable operational expense (opex).

D. Elimination of upfront capital expense (capex) and elimination of variable operational expense (opex).

126. How should a customer forecast the future costs for running a new web application?

A. Amazon Aurora Backtrack

B. Amazon CloudWatch Billing Alarms

C. AWS Simple Monthly Calculator

D. AWS Cost and Usage report

127. Which is the MINIMUM AWS Support plan that provides technical support through phone calls?

A. Enterprise

B. Business

C. Developer

D. Basic

128. Which of the following tasks is the responsibility of AWS?

A. Encrypting client-side data

B. Configuring AWS Identity and Access Management (IAM) roles

C. Securing the Amazon EC2 hypervisor

D. Setting user password policies

129. One benefit of On-Demand Amazon Elastic Compute Cloud (Amazon EC2) pricing is:

A. the ability to bid for a lower hourly cost.

B. paying a daily rate regardless of time used.

C. paying only for time used.

D. pre-paying for instances and paying a lower hourly rate.

130. An administrator needs to rapidly deploy a popular IT solution and start using it immediately. Where can the administrator find assistance?

A. AWS Well-Architected Framework documentation

B. Amazon CloudFront

C. AWS CodeCommit

D. AWS Quick Start reference deployments

131. Which of the following services is in the category of AWS serverless platform?

A. Amazon EMR

B. Elastic Load Balancing

C. AWS Lambda

D. AWS Mobile Hub

132. Which services are parts of the AWS serverless platform?

    A. Amazon EC2, Amazon S3, Amazon Athena
    B. Amazon Kinesis, Amazon SQS, Amazon EMR
    C. AWS Step Functions, Amazon DynamoDB, Amazon SNS
    D. Amazon Athena, Amazon Cognito, Amazon EC2

133. According to the AWS shared responsibility model, what is the sole responsibility of AWS?

    A. Application security
    B. Edge location management
    C. Patch management
    D. Client-side data

134. Which AWS IAM feature is used to associate a set of permissions with multiple users?

    A. Multi-factor authentication
    B. Groups
    C. Password policies
    D. Access keys

135. Which of the following are benefits of the AWS Cloud? (Choose two.)

    A. Unlimited uptime
    B. Elasticity
    C. Agility
    D. Colocation
    E. Capital expenses

136. Which of the following can a customer use to enable single sign-on (SSO) to the AWS Console?

    A. Amazon Connect

    B. AWS Directory Service

    C. Amazon Pinpoint

    D. Amazon Rekognition

137. What are the multiple, isolated locations within an AWS Region that are connected by low-latency networks called?

    A. AWS Direct Connects

    B. Amazon VPCs

    C. Edge locations

    D. Availability Zones

138. Which of the following benefits does the AWS Compliance program provide to AWS customers? (Choose two.)

    A. It verifies that hosted workloads are automatically compliant with the controls of supported compliance frameworks.

    B. AWS is responsible for the maintenance of common compliance framework documentation.

    C. It assures customers that AWS is maintaining physical security and data protection.

    D. It ensures the use of compliance frameworks that are being used by other cloud providers.

    E. It will adopt new compliance frameworks as they become relevant to customer workloads.

139. Which of the following services provides on-demand access to AWS compliance reports?

A. AWS IAM

B. AWS Artifact

C. Amazon GuardDuty

D. AWS KMS

140. As part of the AWS shared responsibility model, which of the following operational controls do users fully inherit from AWS?

A. Security management of data center

B. Patch management

C. Configuration management

D. User and access management

141. When comparing AWS Cloud with on-premises Total Cost of Ownership, which expenses must be considered? (Choose two.)

A. Software development

B. Project management

C. Storage hardware

D. Physical servers

E. Antivirus software license

142. Under the shared responsibility model, which of the following tasks are the responsibility of the customer? (Choose two.)

A. Maintaining the underlying Amazon EC2 hardware.

B. Managing the VPC network access control lists.

C. Encrypting data in transit and at rest.

D. Replacing failed hard disk drives.

E. Deploying hardware in different Availability Zones.

143. Which scenarios represent the concept of elasticity on AWS? (Choose two.)

   A. Scaling the number of Amazon EC2 instances based on trafic.

   B. Resizing Amazon RDS instances as business needs change.

   C. Automatically directing trafic to less-utilized Amazon EC2 instances.

   D. Using AWS compliance documents to accelerate the compliance process.

   E. Having the ability to create and govern environments using code.

144. When is it beneficial for a company to use a Spot Instance?

   A. When there is flexibility in when an application needs to run.

   B. When there are mission-critical workloads.

   C. When dedicated capacity is needed.

   D. When an instance should not be stopped.

145. A company is considering moving its on-premises data center to AWS. What factors should be included in doing a Total Cost of Ownership (TCO) analysis? (Choose two.)

   A. Amazon EC2 instance availability

   B. Power consumption of the data center

   C. Labor costs to replace old servers

   D. Application developer time

   E. Database engine capacity

146. How does AWS charge for AWS Lambda?

    A. Users bid on the maximum price they are willing to pay per hour.

    B. Users choose a 1-, 3- or 5-year upfront payment term.

    C. Users pay for the required permanent storage on a file system or in a database.

    D. Users pay based on the number of requests and consumed compute resources.

147. What function do security groups serve related to Amazon Elastic Compute Cloud (Amazon EC2) instance security?

    A. Act as a virtual firewall for the Amazon EC2 instance.

    B. Secure AWS user accounts with AWS Identity and Access Management (IAM) policies.

    C. Provide DDoS protection with AWS Shield.

    D. Use Amazon CloudFront to protect the Amazon EC2 instance

148. Which disaster recovery scenario offers the lowest probability of down time?

    A. Backup and restore

    B. Pilot light

    C. Warm standby

    D. Multi-site active-active

149. What will help a company perform a cost benefit analysis of migrating to the AWS Cloud?

    A. Cost Explorer

    B. AWS Total Cost of Ownership (TCO) Calculator

    C. AWS Simple Monthly Calculator

    D. AWS Trusted Advisor

150. Which of the following provides the ability to share the cost benefits of Reserved Instances across AWS accounts?

A. AWS Cost Explorer between AWS accounts
B. Linked accounts and consolidated billing
C. Amazon Elastic Compute Cloud (Amazon EC2) Reserved Instance Utilization Report
D. Amazon EC2 Instance Usage Report between AWS accounts

151. A company has multiple AWS accounts and wants to simplify and consolidate its billing process. Which AWS service will achieve this?

A. AWS Cost and Usage Reports
B. AWS Organizations
C. AWS Cost Explorer
D. AWS Budgets

152. A company is designing an application hosted in a single AWS Region serving end-users spread across the world. The company wants to provide the end-users low latency access to the application data. Which of the following services will help fulfill this requirement?

A. Amazon CloudFront
B. AWS Direct Connect
C. Amazon Route 53 global DNS
D. Amazon Simple Storage Service (Amazon S3) transfer acceleration

153. Which of the following deployment models enables customers to fully trade their capital IT expenses for operational expenses?

    A. On-premises
    B. Hybrid
    C. Cloud
    D. Platform as a service

154. How is asset management on AWS easier than asset management in a physical data center?

    A. AWS provides a Configuration Management Database that users can maintain.
    B. AWS performs infrastructure discovery scans on the customer's behalf.
    C. Amazon EC2 automatically generates an asset report and places it in the customer's specified Amazon S3 bucket.
    D. Users can gather asset metadata reliably with a few API calls.

155. What feature of Amazon RDS helps to create globally redundant databases?

    A. Snapshots
    B. Automatic patching and updating
    C. Cross-Region read replicas
    D. Provisioned IOPS

156. Using AWS Identity and Access Management (IAM) to grant access only to the resources needed to perform a task is a concept known as:

A. restricted access.

B. as-needed access.

C. least privilege access.

D. token access.

157. Which methods can be used to identify AWS costs by departments? (Choose two.)

A. Enable multi-factor authentication for the AWS account root user.

B. Create separate accounts for each department.

C. Use Reserved Instances whenever possible.

D. Use tags to associate each instance with a particular department.

E. Pay bills using purchase orders.

158. Under the AWS shared responsibility model, customer responsibilities include which one of the following?

A. Securing the hardware, software, facilities, and networks that run all products and services.

B. Providing certificates, reports, and other documentation directly to AWS customers under NDA.

C. Configuring the operating system, network, and firewall.

D. Obtaining industry certifications and independent third-party attestations.

159. Which managed AWS service provides real-time guidance on AWS security best practices?

    A. AWS X-Ray

    B. AWS Trusted Advisor

    C. Amazon CloudWatch

    D. AWS Systems Manager

160. Which feature adds elasticity to Amazon EC2 instances to handle the changing demand for workloads?

    A. Resource groups

    B. Lifecycle policies

    C. Application Load Balancer

    D. Amazon EC2 Auto Scaling

161. Under the AWS shared responsibility model, customers are responsible for which aspects of security in the cloud? (Choose two.)

    A. Virtualization Management

    B. Hardware management

    C. Encryption management

    D. Facilities management

    E. Firewall management

162. Which AWS hybrid storage service enables your on-premises applications to seamlessly use AWS Cloud storage through standard file-storage protocols?

    A. AWS Direct Connect

    B. AWS Snowball

    C. AWS Storage Gateway

    D. AWS Snowball Edge

163. What is a responsibility of AWS in the shared responsibility model?

    A. Updating the network ACLs to block trafic to vulnerable ports.

    B. Patching operating systems running on Amazon EC2 instances.

    C. Updating the firmware on the underlying EC2 hosts.

    D. Updating the security group rules to block trafic to the vulnerable ports.

164. Which architectural principle is used when deploying an Amazon Relational Database Service (Amazon RDS) instance in Multiple Availability Zone mode?

    A. Implement loose coupling.

    B. Design for failure.

    C. Automate everything that can be automated.

    D. Use services, not servers.

165. What does it mean to grant least privilege to AWS IAM users?

    A. It is granting permissions to a single user only.

    B. It is granting permissions using AWS IAM policies only.

    C. It is granting AdministratorAccess policy permissions to trustworthy users.

    D. It is granting only the permissions required to perform a given task.

166. What is a benefit of loose coupling as a principle of cloud architecture design?

   A. It facilitates low-latency request handling.

   B. It allows applications to have dependent workflows.

   C. It prevents cascading failures between different components.

   D. It allows companies to focus on their physical data center operations.

167. A director has been tasked with investigating hybrid cloud architecture. The company currently accesses AWS over the public internet. Which service will facilitate private hybrid connectivity?

   A. Amazon Virtual Private Cloud (Amazon VPC) NAT Gateway

   B. AWS Direct Connect

   C. Amazon Simple Storage Service (Amazon S3) Transfer Acceleration

   D. AWS Web Application Firewall (AWS WAF)

168. A company's web application currently has tight dependencies on underlying components, so when one component fails the entire web application fails. Applying which AWS Cloud design principle will address the current design issue?

   A. Implementing elasticity, enabling the application to scale up or scale down as demand changes.

   B. Enabling several EC2 instances to run in parallel to achieve better performance.

   C. Focusing on decoupling components by isolating them and ensuring individual components can function when other components fail.

   D. Doubling EC2 computing resources to increase system fault tolerance.

169. How can a customer increase security to AWS account log-ons? (Choose two.)

   A. Configure AWS Certificate Manager
   B. Enable Multi-Factor Authentication (MFA)
   C. Use Amazon Cognito to manage access
   D. Configure a strong password policy
   E. Enable AWS Organizations

170. What AWS service would be used to centrally manage AWS access across multiple accounts?

   A. AWS Service Catalog
   B. AWS Config
   C. AWS Trusted Advisor
   D. AWS Organizations

171. Which AWS service can a customer use to set up an alert notification when the account is approaching a particular dollar amount?

   A. AWS Cost and Usage reports
   B. AWS Budgets
   C. AWS Cost Explorer
   D. AWS Trusted Advisor

172. What can users access from AWS Artifact?

   A. AWS security and compliance documents
   B. A download of configuration management details for all AWS resources
   C. Training materials for AWS services
   D. A security assessment of the applications deployed in the AWS Cloud

173. What is the MINIMUM AWS Support plan that provides designated Technical Account Managers?

A. Enterprise

B. Business

C. Developer

D. Basic

174. Which of the following is an AWS Well-Architected Framework design principle related to reliability?

A. Deployment to a single Availability Zone

B. Ability to recover from failure

C. Design for cost optimization

D. Perform operations as code

175. Which type of AWS storage is ephemeral and is deleted when an instance is stopped or terminated?

A. Amazon EBS

B. Amazon EC2 instance store

C. Amazon EFS

D. Amazon S3

176. What is an advantage of using the AWS Cloud over a traditional on-premises solution?

A. Users do not have to guess about future capacity needs.

B. Users can utilize existing hardware contracts for purchases.

C. Users can fix costs no matter what their trafic is.

D. Users can avoid audits by using reports from AWS.

177. Which of the following is an AWS-managed compute service?

   A. Amazon SWF
   B. Amazon EC2
   C. AWS Lambda
   D. Amazon Aurora

178. Which of the following is an important architectural principle when designing cloud applications?

   A. Store data and backups in the same region.
   B. Design tightly coupled system components.
   C. Avoid multi-threading.
   D. Design for failure.

179. Which mechanism allows developers to access AWS services from application code?

   A. AWS Software Development Kit
   B. AWS Management Console
   C. AWS CodePipeline
   D. AWS Config

180. Which Amazon EC2 pricing model is the MOST cost eficient for an uninterruptible workload that runs once a year for 24 hours?

   A. On-Demand Instances
   B. Reserved Instances
   C. Spot Instances
   D. Dedicated Instances

181. Which of the following services is a MySQL-compatible database that automatically grows storage as needed?

   A. Amazon Elastic Compute Cloud (Amazon EC2)
   B. Amazon Relational Database Service (Amazon RDS) for MySQL
   C. Amazon Lightsail
   D. Amazon Aurora

182. Which Amazon Virtual Private Cloud (Amazon VPC) feature enables users to connect two VPCs together?

   A. Amazon VPC endpoints
   B. Amazon Elastic Compute Cloud (Amazon EC2) Classi-cLink
   C. Amazon VPC peering
   D. AWS Direct Connect

183. Which service's PRIMARY purpose is software version control?

   A. Amazon CodeStar
   B. AWS Command Line Interface (AWS CLI)
   C. Amazon Cognito
   D. AWS CodeCommit

184. A company is considering migrating its applications to AWS. The company wants to compare the cost of running the workload on-premises to running the equivalent workload on the AWS platform. Which tool can be used to perform this comparison?

   A. AWS Simple Monthly Calculator
   B. AWS Total Cost of Ownership (TCO) Calculator
   C. AWS Billing and Cost Management console
   D. Cost Explorer

185. Which AWS service provides a secure, fast, and cost-effective way to migrate or transport exabyte-scale datasets into AWS?

    A. AWS Batch
    B. AWS Snowball
    C. AWS Migration Hub
    D. AWS Snowmobile

186. Which of the following BEST describe the AWS pricing model? (Choose two.)

    A. Fixed-term
    B. Pay-as-you-go
    C. Colocation
    D. Planned
    E. Variable cost

187. Which load balancer types are available with Elastic Load Balancing (ELB)? (Choose two.)

    A. Public load balancers with AWS Application Auto Scaling capabilities
    B. F5 Big-IP and Citrix NetScaler load balancers
    C. Classic Load Balancers
    D. Cross-zone load balancers with public and private IPs
    E. Application Load Balancers

188. Why should a company choose AWS instead of a traditional data center?

   A. AWS provides users with full control over the underlying resources.

   B. AWS does not require long-term contracts and provides a pay-as-you-go model.

   C. AWS offers edge locations in every country, supporting global reach.

   D. AWS has no limits on the number of resources that can be created.

189. Which solution provides the FASTEST application response times to frequently accessed data to users in multiple AWS Regions?

   A. AWS CloudTrail across multiple Availability Zones

   B. Amazon CloudFront to edge locations

   C. AWS CloudFormation in multiple regions

   D. A virtual private gateway over AWS Direct Connect

190. Which AWS service provides a self-service portal for on-demand access to AWS compliance reports?

   A. AWS Config

   B. AWS Certificate Manager

   C. Amazon Inspector

   D. AWS Artifact

191. Which of the following AWS services can be used to run a self-managed database?

   A. Amazon Route 53

   B. AWS X-Ray

   C. AWS Snowmobile

   D. Amazon Elastic Compute Cloud (Amazon EC2)

192. What exclusive benefit is provided to users with Enterprise Support?

   A. Access to a Technical Project Manager
   B. Access to a Technical Account Manager
   C. Access to a Cloud Support Engineer
   D. Access to a Solutions Architect

193. How can a user protect against AWS service disruptions if a natural disaster affects an entire geographic area?

   A. Deploy applications across multiple Availability Zones within an AWS Region.
   B. Use a hybrid cloud computing deployment model within the geographic area.
   C. Deploy applications across multiple AWS Regions.
   D. Store application artifacts using AWS Artifact and replicate them across multiple AWS Regions.

194. How does AWS MOST effectively reduce computing costs for a growing start-up company?

   A. It provides on-demand resources for peak usage.
   B. It automates the provisioning of individual developer environments.
   C. It automates customer relationship management.
   D. It implements a fixed monthly computing budget.

195. A startup is working on a new application that needs to go to market quickly. The application requirements may need to be adjusted in the near future. Which of the following is a characteristic of the AWS Cloud that would meet this specific need?

   A. Elasticity
   B. Reliability
   C. Performance
   D. Agility

196. Which AWS Support plan provides a full set of AWS Trusted Advisor checks?

   A. Business and Developer Support
   B. Business and Basic Support
   C. Enterprise and Developer Support
   D. Enterprise and Business Support

197. Which of the following services have Distributed Denial of Service (DDoS) mitigation features? (Choose two.)

   A. AWS WAF
   B. Amazon DynamoDB
   C. Amazon EC2
   D. Amazon CloudFront
   E. Amazon Inspector

198. When building a cloud Total Cost of Ownership (TCO) model, which cost elements should be considered for workloads running on AWS? (Choose three.)

    A. Compute costs
    B. Facilities costs
    C. Storage costs
    D. Data transfer costs
    E. Network infrastructure costs
    F. Hardware lifecycle costs

199. What time-savings advantage is offered with the use of Amazon Rekognition?

    A. Amazon Rekognition provides automatic watermarking of images.
    B. Amazon Rekognition provides automatic detection of objects appearing in pictures.
    C. Amazon Rekognition provides the ability to resize millions of images automatically.
    D. Amazon Rekognition uses Amazon Mechanical Turk to allow humans to bid on object detection jobs.

200. When comparing AWS with on-premises Total Cost of Ownership (TCO), what costs are included?

    A. Data center security
    B. Business analysis
    C. Project management
    D. Operating system administration

201. According to the AWS shared responsibility model, what is AWS responsible for?

   A. Configuring Amazon VPC
   B. Managing application code
   C. Maintaining application trafic
   D. Managing the network infrastructure

202. Which service should be used to estimate the costs of running a new project on AWS?

   A. AWS TCO Calculator
   B. AWS Simple Monthly Calculator
   C. AWS Cost Explorer API
   D. AWS Budgets

203. Which AWS tool will identify security groups that grant unrestricted Internet access to a limited list of ports?

   A. AWS Organizations
   B. AWS Trusted Advisor
   C. AWS Usage Report
   D. Amazon EC2 dashboard

204. Which AWS service can be used to generate alerts based on an estimated monthly bill?

   A. AWS Config
   B. Amazon CloudWatch
   C. AWS X-Ray
   D. AWS CloudTrail

205. Which Amazon EC2 pricing model offers the MOST significant discount when compared to On-Demand Instances?

   A. Partial Upfront Reserved Instances for a 1-year term
   B. All Upfront Reserved Instances for a 1-year term
   C. All Upfront Reserved Instances for a 3-year term
   D. No Upfront Reserved Instances for a 3-year term

206. Which of the following is the responsibility of AWS?

   A. Setting up AWS Identity and Access Management (IAM) users and groups
   B. Physically destroying storage media at end of life
   C. Patching guest operating systems
   D. Configuring security settings on Amazon EC2 instances

207. Which of the following is an advantage of using AWS?

   A. AWS audits user data.
   B. Data is automatically secure.
   C. There is no guessing on capacity needs.
   D. AWS manages compliance needs.

208. Which AWS service would a customer use with a static website to achieve lower latency and high transfer speeds?

   A. AWS Lambda
   B. Amazon DynamoDB Accelerator
   C. Amazon Route 53
   D. Amazon CloudFront

209. Which services manage and automate application deployments on AWS? (Choose two.)

   A. AWS Elastic Beanstalk
   B. AWS CodeCommit
   C. AWS Data Pipeline
   D. AWS CloudFormation
   E. AWS Config

210. A user wants guidance on possible savings when migrating from on-premises to AWS. Which tool is suitable for this scenario?

   A. AWS Budgets
   B. Cost Explorer
   C. AWS Total Cost of Ownership (TCO) Calculator
   D. AWS Well-Architected Tool

211. Which principles are used to architect applications for reliability on the AWS Cloud? (Choose two.)

   A. Design for automated failure recovery
   B. Use multiple Availability Zones
   C. Manage changes via documented processes
   D. Test for moderate demand to ensure reliability
   E. Backup recovery to an on-premises environment

212. What tasks should a customer perform when that customer suspects an AWS account has been compromised? (Choose two.)

   A. Rotate passwords and access keys.
   B. Remove MFA tokens.
   C. Move resources to a different AWS Region.
   D. Delete AWS CloudTrail Resources.
   E. Contact AWS Support.

213. What is an example of high availability in the AWS Cloud?

    A. Consulting AWS technical support at any time day or night

    B. Ensuring an application remains accessible, even if a resource fails

    C. Making any AWS service available for use by paying on demand

    D. Deploying in any part of the world using AWS Regions

214. Which AWS security service protects applications from distributed denial of service attacks with always-on detection and automatic inline mitigations?

    A. Amazon Inspector

    B. AWS Web Application Firewall (AWS WAF)

    C. Elastic Load Balancing (ELB)

    D. AWS Shield

215. A company wants to monitor the CPU usage of its Amazon EC2 resources. Which AWS service should the company use?

    A. AWS CloudTrail

    B. Amazon CloudWatch

    C. AWS Cost and Usage report

    D. Amazon Simple Notification Service (Amazon SNS)

216. What is an AWS Identity and Access Management (IAM) role?

    A. A user associated with an AWS resource

    B. A group associated with an AWS resource

    C. An entity that defines a set of permissions for use with an AWS resource

    D. An authentication credential associated with a multi-factor authentication (MFA) token

217. What are the advantages of Reserved Instances? (Choose two.)

   A. They provide a discount over on-demand pricing.
   B. They provide access to additional instance types.
   C. They provide additional networking capability.
   D. Customers can upgrade instances as new types become available.
   E. Customers can reserve capacity in an Availability Zone.

218. How do Amazon EC2 Auto Scaling groups help achieve high availability for a web application?

   A. They automatically add more instances across multiple AWS Regions based on global demand of the application.
   B. They automatically add or replace instances across multiple Availability Zones when the application needs it.
   C. They enable the application's static content to reside closer to end users.
   D. They are able to distribute incoming requests across a tier of web server instances.

219. How can one AWS account use Reserved Instances from another AWS account?

   A. By using Amazon EC2 Dedicated Instances
   B. By using AWS Organizations consolidated billing
   C. By using the AWS Cost Explorer tool
   D. By using AWS Budgets

220. A customer runs an On-Demand Amazon Linux EC2 instance for 3 hours, 5 minutes, and 6 seconds. For how much time will the customer be billed?

A. 3 hours, 5 minutes

B. 3 hours, 5 minutes, and 6 seconds

C. 3 hours, 6 minutes

D. 4 hours

221. Which of the following AWS services provide compute resources? (Choose two.)

A. AWS Lambda

B. Amazon Elastic Container Service (Amazon ECS)

C. AWS CodeDeploy

D. Amazon Glacier

E. AWS Organizations

222. Which AWS service enables users to deploy infrastructure as code by automating the process of provisioning resources?

A. Amazon GameLift

B. AWS CloudFormation

C. AWS Data Pipeline

D. AWS Glue

223. Which AWS services provide a way to extend an on-premises architecture to the AWS Cloud? (Choose two.)

A. Amazon EBS

B. AWS Direct Connect

C. Amazon CloudFront

D. AWS Storage Gateway

E. Amazon Connect

224. Which of the following allows users to provision a dedicated network connection from their internal network to AWS?

    A. AWS CloudHSM
    B. AWS Direct Connect
    C. AWS VPN
    D. Amazon Connect

225. Which services use AWS edge locations? (Choose two.)

    A. Amazon CloudFront
    B. AWS Shield
    C. Amazon EC2
    D. Amazon RDS
    E. Amazon ElastiCache

226. Which service would provide network connectivity in a hybrid architecture that includes the AWS Cloud?

    A. Amazon VPC
    B. AWS Direct Connect
    C. AWS Directory Service
    D. Amazon API Gateway

227. Which tool can be used to compare the costs of running a web application in a traditional hosting environment to running it on AWS?

    A. AWS Cost Explorer
    B. AWS Budgets
    C. AWS Cost and Usage report
    D. AWS Total Cost of Ownership (TCO) Calculator

228. What is the value of using third-party software from AWS Marketplace instead of installing third-party software on Amazon EC2? (Choose two.)

    A. Users pay for software by the hour or month depending on licensing.
    B. AWS Marketplace enables the user to launch applications with 1-Click.
    C. AWS Marketplace data encryption is managed by a third-party vendor.
    D. AWS Marketplace eliminates the need to upgrade to newer software versions.
    E. Users can deploy third-party software without testing.

229. Which of the following is a cloud architectural design principle?

    A. Scale up, not out.
    B. Loosely couple components.
    C. Build monolithic systems.
    D. Use commercial database software.

230. Under the shared responsibility model; which of the following areas are the customer's responsibility? (Choose two.)

    A. Firmware upgrades of network infrastructure
    B. Patching of operating systems
    C. Patching of the underlying hypervisor
    D. Physical security of data centers
    E. Configuration of the security group

231. Which service enables customers to audit and monitor changes in AWS resources?

  A. AWS Trusted Advisor
  B. Amazon GuardDuty
  C. Amazon Inspector
  D. AWS Config

232. Which AWS service identifies security groups that allow unrestricted access to a user's AWS resources?

  A. AWS CloudTrail
  B. AWS Trusted Advisor
  C. Amazon CloudWatch
  D. Amazon Inspector

233. According to the AWS shared responsibility model, who is responsible for configuration management?

  A. It is solely the responsibility of the customer.
  B. It is solely the responsibility of AWS.
  C. It is shared between AWS and the customer.
  D. It is not part of the AWS shared responsibility model.

234. Which AWS service is a content delivery network that securely delivers data, video, and applications to users globally with low latency and high speeds?

  A. AWS CloudFormation
  B. AWS Direct Connect
  C. Amazon CloudFront
  D. Amazon Pinpoint

235. Which benefit of the AWS Cloud supports matching the supply of resources with changing workload demands?

   A. Security
   B. Reliability
   C. Elasticity
   D. High availability

236. A user is running an application on AWS and notices that one or more AWS-owned IP addresses is involved in a distributed denial-of-service (DDoS) attack. Who should the user contact FIRST about this situation?

   A. AWS Premium Support
   B. AWS Technical Account Manager
   C. AWS Solutions Architect
   D. AWS Abuse team

237. Which of the following are benefits of hosting infrastructure in the AWS Cloud? (Choose two.)

   A. There are no upfront commitments.
   B. AWS manages all security in the cloud.
   C. Users have the ability to provision resources on demand.
   D. Users have access to free and unlimited storage.
   E. Users have control over the physical infrastructure.

238. Access keys in AWS Identity and Access Management (IAM) are used to:

   A. log in to the AWS Management Console.
   B. make programmatic calls to AWS from AWS APIs.
   C. log in to Amazon EC2 instances.
   D. authenticate to AWS CodeCommit repositories.

239. What is AWS Trusted Advisor?

    A. It is an AWS staff member who provides recommendations and best practices on how to use AWS.

    B. It is a network of AWS partners who provide recommendations and best practices on how to use AWS.

    C. It is an online tool with a set of automated checks that provides recommendations on cost optimization, performance, and security.

    D. It is another name for AWS Technical Account Managers who provide recommendations on cost optimization, performance, and security.

240. Which AWS service or feature allows a company to visualize, understand, and manage AWS costs and usage over time?

    A. AWS Budgets

    B. AWS Cost Explorer

    C. AWS Organizations

    D. Consolidated billing

241. Which AWS service offers on-demand access to AWS security and compliance reports?

    A. AWS CloudTrail

    B. AWS Artifact

    C. AWS Health

    D. Amazon CloudWatch

242. What are the benefits of using the AWS Cloud for companies with customers in many countries around the world? (Choose two.)

 A. Companies can deploy applications in multiple AWS Regions to reduce latency.
 B. Amazon Translate automatically translates third-party website interfaces into multiple languages.
 C. Amazon CloudFront has multiple edge locations around the world to reduce latency.
 D. Amazon Comprehend allows users to build applications that can respond to user requests in many languages.
 E. Elastic Load Balancing can distribute application web trafic to multiple AWS Regions around the world, which reduces latency.

243. Which AWS service handles the deployment details of capacity provisioning, load balancing, Auto Scaling, and application health monitoring?

 A. AWS Config
 B. AWS Elastic Beanstalk
 C. Amazon Route 53
 D. Amazon CloudFront

244. Which AWS service provides inbound and outbound network ACLs to harden external connectivity to Amazon EC2?

 A. AWS IAM
 B. Amazon Connect
 C. Amazon VPC
 D. Amazon API Gateway

245. When a company provisions web servers in multiple AWS Regions, what is being increased?

A. Coupling
B. Availability
C. Security
D. Durability

246. The pay-as-you-go pricing model for AWS services:

A. reduces capital expenditures.
B. requires payment up front for AWS services.
C. is relevant only for Amazon EC2, Amazon S3, and Amazon RDS.
D. reduces operational expenditures.

247. Under the AWS shared responsibility model, AWS is responsible for which security-related task?

A. Lifecycle management of IAM credentials
B. Physical security of global infrastructure
C. Encryption of Amazon EBS volumes
D. Firewall configuration

248. Which AWS service enables users to consolidate billing across multiple accounts?

A. Amazon QuickSight
B. AWS Organizations
C. AWS Budgets
D. Amazon Forecast

249. Under the AWS shared responsibility model, which of the following is an example of security in the AWS Cloud?

A. Managing edge locations

B. Physical security

C. Firewall configuration

D. Global infrastructure

250. How can an AWS user with an AWS Basic Support plan obtain technical assistance from AWS?

A. AWS Senior Support Engineers

B. AWS Technical Account Managers

C. AWS Trusted Advisor

D. AWS Discussion Forums

251. Which of the following are pillars of the AWS Well-Architected Framework? (Choose two.)

A. Multiple Availability Zones

B. Performance efficiency

C. Security

D. Encryption usage

E. High availability

252. After selecting an Amazon EC2 Dedicated Host reservation, which pricing option would provide the largest discount?

A. No upfront payment

B. Hourly on-demand payment

C. Partial upfront payment

D. All upfront payment

253. What is an advantage of deploying an application across multiple Availability Zones?

   A. There is a lower risk of service failure if a natural disaster causes a service disruption in a given AWS Region.

   B. The application will have higher availability because it can withstand a service disruption in one Availability Zone.

   C. There will be better coverage as Availability Zones are geographically distant and can serve a wider area.

   D. There will be decreased application latency that will improve the user experience.

254. A Cloud Practitioner is asked how to estimate the cost of using a new application on AWS. What is the MOST appropriate response?

   A. Inform the user that AWS pricing allows for on-demand pricing.

   B. Direct the user to the AWS Simple Monthly Calculator for an estimate.

   C. Use Amazon QuickSight to analyze current spending on-premises.

   D. Use Amazon AppStream 2.0 for real-time pricing analytics.

255. A company wants to migrate its applications to a VPC on AWS. These applications will need to access on-premises resources. What combination of actions will enable the company to accomplish this goal? (Choose two.)

A. Use the AWS Service Catalog to identify a list of on-premises resources that can be migrated.

B. Build a VPN connection between an on-premises device and a virtual private gateway in the new VPC.

C. Use Amazon Athena to query data from the on-premises database servers.

D. Connect the company›s on-premises data center to AWS using AWS Direct Connect.

E. Leverage Amazon CloudFront to restrict access to static web content provided through the company›s on-premises web servers.

256. A web application running on AWS has been spammed with malicious requests from a recurring set of IP addresses. Which AWS service can help secure the application and block the malicious traffic?

A. AWS IAM

B. Amazon GuardDuty

C. Amazon Simple Notification Service (Amazon SNS)

D. AWS WAF

257. Treating infrastructure as code in the AWS Cloud allows users to:

A. automate migration of on-premises hardware to AWS data centers.

B. let a third party automate an audit of the AWS infrastructure.

C. turn over application code to AWS so it can run on the AWS infrastructure.

D. automate the infrastructure provisioning process.

258. A company requires a dedicated network connection between its on-premises servers and the AWS Cloud. Which AWS service should be used?

A. AWS VPN

B. AWS Direct Connect

C. Amazon API Gateway

D. Amazon Connect

259. Which AWS service can be used to query stored datasets directly from Amazon S3 using standard SQL?

A. AWS Glue

B. AWS Data Pipeline

C. Amazon CloudSearch

D. Amazon Athena

260. AWS CloudFormation is designed to help the user:

A. model and provision resources.

B. update application code.

C. set up data lakes.

D. create reports for billing.

261. Which of the following is an AWS database service?

   A. Amazon Redshift

   B. Amazon Elastic Block Store (Amazon EBS)

   C. Amazon S3 Glacier

   D. AWS Snowball

262. A Cloud Practitioner must determine if any security groups in an AWS account have been provisioned to allow unrestricted access for specific ports. What is the SIMPLEST way to do this?

   A. Review the inbound rules for each security group in the Amazon EC2 management console to check for port 0.0.0.0/0.

   B. Run AWS Trusted Advisor and review the findings.

   C. Open the AWS IAM console and check the inbound rule filters for open access.

   D. In AWS Config, create a custom rule that invokes an AWS Lambda function to review rules for inbound access.

263. What are the benefits of developing and running a new application in the AWS Cloud compared to on-premises? (Choose two.)

   A. AWS automatically distributes the data globally for higher durability.

   B. AWS will take care of operating the application.

   C. AWS makes it easy to architect for high availability.

   D. AWS can easily accommodate application demand changes.

   E. AWS takes care application security patching.

264. A user needs an automated security assessment report that will identify unintended network access to Amazon EC2 instances and vulnerabilities on those instances. Which AWS service will provide this assessment report?

A. EC2 security groups

B. AWS Config

C. Amazon Macie

D. Amazon Inspector

265. How can a company isolate the costs of production and non-production workloads on AWS?

A. Create Identity and Access Management (IAM) roles for production and non-production workloads.

B. Use different accounts for production and non-production expenses.

C. Use Amazon EC2 for non-production workloads and other services for production workloads.

D. Use Amazon CloudWatch to monitor the use of services.

266. Where can users find a catalog of AWS-recognized providers of third-party security solutions?

A. AWS Service Catalog

B. AWS Marketplace

C. AWS Quick Start

D. AWS CodeDeploy

267. A Cloud Practitioner needs to store data for 7 years to meet regulatory requirements. Which AWS service will meet this requirement at the LOWEST cost?

   A. Amazon S3
   B. AWS Snowball
   C. Amazon Redshift
   D. Amazon S3 Glacier

268. What are the immediate benefits of using the AWS Cloud? (Choose two.)

   A. Increased IT staff.
   B. Capital expenses are replaced with variable expenses.
   C. User control of infrastructure.
   D. Increased agility.
   E. AWS holds responsibility for security in the cloud.

269. Which security service automatically recognizes and classifies sensitive data or intellectual property on AWS?

   A. Amazon GuardDuty
   B. Amazon Macie
   C. Amazon Inspector
   D. AWS Shield

270. What is the purpose of AWS Storage Gateway?

   A. It ensures on-premises data storage is 99.999999999% durable.
   B. It transports petabytes of data to and from AWS.
   C. It connects to multiple Amazon EC2 instances.
   D. It connects on-premises data storage to the AWS Cloud.

271. What should users do if they want to install an application in geographically isolated locations?

   A. Install the application using multiple internet gateways.
   B. Deploy the application to an Amazon VPC.
   C. Deploy the application to multiple AWS Regions.
   D. Configure the application using multiple NAT gateways.

272. A system in the AWS Cloud is designed to withstand the failure of one or more components. What is this an example of?

   A. Elasticity
   B. High Availability
   C. Scalability
   D. Agility

273. A Cloud Practitioner needs a consistent and dedicated connection between AWS resources and an on-premises system. Which AWS service can fulfill this requirement?

   A. AWS Direct Connect
   B. AWS VPN
   C. Amazon Connect
   D. AWS Data Pipeline

274. Within the AWS shared responsibility model, who is responsible for security and compliance?

   A. The customer is responsible.
   B. AWS is responsible.
   C. AWS and the customer share responsibility.
   D. AWS shares responsibility with the relevant governing body.

275. To use the AWS CLI, users are required to generate:

    A. a password policy.
    B. an access/secret key.
    C. a managed policy.
    D. an API key.

276. Which AWS service is used to provide encryption for Amazon EBS?

    A. AWS Certificate Manager
    B. AWS Systems Manager
    C. AWS KMS
    D. AWS Config

277. How does AWS charge for AWS Lambda usage once the free tier has been exceeded? (Choose two.)

    A. By the time it takes for the Lambda function to execute.
    B. By the number of versions of a specific Lambda function.
    C. By the number of requests made for a given Lambda function.
    D. By the programming language that is used for the Lambda function.
    E. By the total number of Lambda functions in an AWS account.

278. Which of the following describes the relationships among AWS Regions, Availability Zones, and edge locations? (Choose two.)

    A. There are more AWS Regions than Availability Zones.
    B. There are more edge locations than AWS Regions.
    C. An edge location is an Availability Zone.
    D. There are more AWS Regions than edge locations.
    E. There are more Availability Zones than AWS Regions.

279. What does AWS Shield Standard provide?

    A. WAF rules

    B. DDoS protection

    C. Identity and Access Management (IAM) permissions and access to resources

    D. Data encryption

280. A company wants to build its new application workloads in the AWS Cloud instead of using on-premises resources. What expense can be reduced using the AWS Cloud?

    A. The cost of writing custom-built Java or Node .js code

    B. Penetration testing for security

    C. hardware required to support new applications

    D. Writing specific test cases for third-party applications.

281. What does AWS Marketplace allow users to do? (Choose two.)

    A. Sell unused Amazon EC2 Spot Instances.

    B. Sell solutions to other AWS users.

    C. Buy third-party software that runs on AWS.

    D. Purchase AWS security and compliance documents.

    E. Order AWS Snowball.

282. What does it mean if a user deploys a hybrid cloud architecture on AWS?

    A. All resources run using on-premises infrastructure.

    B. Some resources run on-premises and some run in a colocation center.

    C. All resources run in the AWS Cloud.

    D. Some resources run on-premises and some run in the AWS Cloud.

283. Which AWS service allows users to identify the changes made to a resource over time?

    A. Amazon Inspector
    B. AWS Config
    C. AWS Service Catalog
    D. AWS IAM

284. How can a company reduce its Total Cost of Ownership (TCO) using AWS?

    A. By minimizing large capital expenditures
    B. By having no responsibility for third-party license costs
    C. By having no operational expenditures
    D. By having AWS manage applications

285. Which activity is a customer responsibility in the AWS Cloud according to the AWS shared responsibility model?

    A. Ensuring network connectivity from AWS to the internet
    B. Patching and fixing flaws within the AWS Cloud infrastructure
    C. Ensuring the physical security of cloud data centers
    D. Ensuring Amazon EBS volumes are backed up

286. What are the advantages of the AWS Cloud? (Choose two.)

    A. Fixed rate monthly cost
    B. No need to guess capacity requirements
    C. Increased speed to market
    D. Increased upfront capital expenditure
    E. Physical access to cloud data centers

287. When comparing the total cost of ownership (TCO) of an on-premises infrastructure to a cloud architecture, what costs should be considered? (Choose two.)

   A. The credit card processing fees for application transactions in the cloud.
   B. The cost of purchasing and installing server hardware in the on-premises data.
   C. The cost of administering the infrastructure, including operating system and software installations, patches, backups, and recovering from failures.
   D. The costs of third-party penetration testing.
   E. The advertising costs associated with an ongoing enterprise-wide campaign.

288. Which AWS feature allows a company to take advantage of usage tiers for services across multiple member accounts?

   A. Service control policies (SCPs)
   B. Consolidated billing
   C. All Upfront Reserved Instances
   D. AWS Cost Explorer

289. What is one of the customer's responsibilities according to the AWS shared responsibility model?

   A. Virtualization infrastructure
   B. Network infrastructure
   C. Application security
   D. Physical security of hardware

290. What helps a company provide a lower latency experience to its users globally?

   A. Using an AWS Region that is central to all users
   B. Using a second Availability Zone in the AWS Region that is using used
   C. Enabling caching in the AWS Region that is being used
   D. Using edge locations to put content closer to all users

291. How can the AWS Cloud increase user workforce productivity after migration from an on-premises data center?

   A. Users do not have to wait for infrastructure provisioning.
   B. The AWS Cloud infrastructure is much faster than an on-premises data center infrastructure.
   C. AWS takes over application configuration management on behalf of users.
   D. Users do not need to address security and compliance issues.

292. Which AWS service provides a quick and automated way to create and manage AWS accounts?

   A. AWS QuickSight
   B. Amazon Lightsail
   C. AWS Organizations
   D. Amazon Connect

293. Which Amazon RDS feature can be used to achieve high availability?

   A. Multiple Availability Zones
   B. Amazon Reserved Instances
   C. Provisioned IOPS storage
   D. Enhanced monitoring

294. Where should users report that AWS resources are being used for malicious purposes?

A. AWS Abuse team
B. AWS Shield
C. AWS Support
D. AWS Developer Forums

295. Which AWS service needs to be enabled to track all user account changes within the AWS Management Console?

A. AWS CloudTrail
B. Amazon Simple Notification Service (Amazon SNS)
C. VPC Flow Logs
D. AWS CloudHSM

296. What is an AWS Cloud design best practice?

A. Tight coupling of components
B. Single point of failure
C. High availability
D. Overprovisioning of resources

297. Which of the following is an example of how moving to the AWS Cloud reduces upfront cost?

A. By replacing large variable costs with lower capital investments
B. By replacing large capital investments with lower variable costs
C. By allowing the provisioning of compute and storage at a fixed level to meet peak demand
D. By replacing the repeated scaling of virtual servers with a simpler fixed-scale model

298. When designing a typical three-tier web application, which AWS services and/or features improve availability and reduce the impact failures? (Choose two.)

A. AWS Auto Scaling for Amazon EC2 instances

B. Amazon VPC subnet ACLs to check the health of a service

C. Distributed resources across multiple Availability Zones

D. AWS Server Migration Service (AWS SMS) to move Amazon EC2 instances into a different Region

E. Distributed resources across multiple AWS points of presence

299. Which cloud design principle aligns with AWS Cloud best practices?

A. Create fixed dependencies among application components

B. Aggregate services on a single instance

C. Deploy applications in a single Availability Zone

D. Distribute the compute load across multiple resources

300. Which of the following are recommended practices for managing IAM users? (Choose two.)

A. Require IAM users to change their passwords after a specified period of time

B. Prevent IAM users from reusing previous passwords

C. Recommend that the same password be used on AWS and other sites

D. Require IAM users to store their passwords in raw text

E. Disable multi-factor authentication (MFA) for IAM users

301. A company is migrating from on-premises data centers to the AWS Cloud and is looking for hands-on help with the project. How can the company get this support? (Choose two.)

   A. Ask for a quote from the AWS Marketplace team to perform a migration into the company›s AWS account.

   B. Contact AWS Support and open a case for assistance

   C. Use AWS Professional Services to provide guidance and to set up an AWS Landing Zone in the company›s AWS account

   D. Select a partner from the AWS Partner Network (APN) to assist with the migration

   E. Use Amazon Connect to create a new request for proposal (RFP) for expert assistance in migrating to the AWS Cloud.

302. How does the AWS Enterprise Support Concierge team help users?

   A. Supporting application development

   B. Providing architecture guidance

   C. Answering billing and account inquires

   D. Answering questions regarding technical support cases

303. An application designed to span multiple Availability Zones is described as:

   A. being highly available

   B. having global reach

   C. using an economy of scale

   D. having elasticity

304. A new service using AWS must be highly available. Yet, due to regulatory requirements, all of its Amazon EC2 instances must be located in a single geographic area. According to best practices, to meet these requirements, the EC2 instances must be placed in at least two:

   A. AWS Regions
   B. Availability Zones
   C. subnets
   D. placement groups

305. Which AWS tool is used to compare the cost of running an application on-premises to running the application in the AWS Cloud?

   A. AWS Trusted Advisor
   B. AWS Simple Monthly Calculator
   C. AWS Total Cost of Ownership (TCO) Calculator
   D. Cost Explorer

306. A company has multiple AWS accounts within AWS Organizations and wants to apply the Amazon EC2 Reserved Instances benefit to a single account only.

   A. Purchase the Reserved Instances from master payer account and turn off Reserved Instance sharing.
   B. Enable billing alerts in the AWS Billing and Cost Management console.
   C. Purchase the Reserved Instances in individual linked accounts and turn off Reserved Instance sharing from the payer level.
   D. Enable Reserved Instance sharing in the AWS Billing and Cost Management console.

307. Which situation should be reported to the AWS Abuse team?

   A. In Availability Zone has a service disruption
   B. An intrusion attempt is made from an AWS IP address
   C. A user has trouble accessing an Amazon S3 bucket from an AWS IP address
   D. A user needs to change payment methods due to a compromise

308. A company is planning to launch an ecommerce site in a single AWS Region to a worldwide user base. Which AWS services will allow the company to reach users and provide low latency and high transfer speeds? (Choose two.)

   A. Application Load Balancer
   B. AWS Global Accelerator
   C. AWS Direct Connect
   D. Amazon CloudFront
   E. AWS Lambda

309. Which AWS service or resource is serverless?

   A. AWS Lambda
   B. Amazon EC2 instances
   C. Amazon Lightsail
   D. Amazon ElastiCache

310. Which of the following are components of Amazon VPC? (Choose two.)

   A. Objects
   B. Subnets
   C. Buckets
   D. Internet gateways
   E. Access key

311. AWS Budgets can be used to:

   A. prevent a given user from creating a resource
   B. send an alert when the utilization of Reserved Instances drops below a certain percentage
   C. set resource limits in AWS accounts to prevent over-spending
   D. split an AWS bill across multiple forms of payment

312. Which of the following will enhance the security of access to the AWS Management Console? (Choose two.)

   A. AWS Secrets Manager
   B. AWS Certificate Manager
   C. AWS Multi-Factor Authentication (AWS MFA)
   D. Security groups
   E. Password policies

313. The AWS Trusted Advisor checks include recommendations regarding which of the following? (Choose two.)

   A. Information on Amazon S3 bucket permissions
   B. AWS service outages
   C. Multi-factor authentication enabled on the AWS account root user
   D. Available software patches
   E. Number of users in the account

314. Which functions can users perform using AWS KMS?

   A. Create and manage AWS access keys for the AWS account root user

   B. Create and manage AWS access keys for an AWS account IAM user

   C. Create and manage keys for encryption and decryption of data

   D. Create and manage keys for multi-factor authentication

315. How does AWS Trusted Advisor provide guidance to users of the AWS Cloud? (Choose two.)

   A. It identifies software vulnerabilities in applications running on AWS

   B. It provides a list of cost optimization recommendations based on current AWS usage

   C. It detects potential security vulnerabilities caused by permissions settings on account resources

   D. It automatically corrects potential security issues caused by permissions settings on account resources

   E. It provides proactive alerting whenever an Amazon EC2 instance has been compromised

316. Which of the following are advantages of the AWS Cloud? (Choose two.)

   A. AWS manages the maintenance of the cloud infrastructure

   B. AWS manages the security of applications built on AWS

   C. AWS manages capacity planning for physical servers

   D. AWS manages the development of applications on AWS

   E. AWS manages cost planning for virtual servers

317. A user deploys an Amazon RDS DB instance in multiple Availability Zones. This strategy involves which pillar of the AWS Well-Architected Framework?

    A. Performance eficiency
    B. Reliability
    C. Cost optimization
    D. Security

318. Which AWS services provide a user with connectivity between the AWS Cloud and on-premises resources? (Choose two.)

    A. AWS VPN
    B. Amazon Connect
    C. Amazon Cognito
    D. AWS Direct Connect
    E. AWS Managed Services

319. Which AWS service is used to pay AWS bills, and monitor usage and budget costs?

    A. AWS Billing and Cost Management
    B. Consolidated billing
    C. Amazon CloudWatch
    D. Amazon QuickSight

320. Which element of the AWS global infrastructure consists of one or more discrete data centers, each with redundant power, networking, and connectivity, which are housed in separate facilities?

    A. AWS Regions
    B. Availability Zones
    C. Edge locations
    D. Amazon CloudFront

321. Which Amazon VPC feature enables users to capture information about the IP trafic that reaches Amazon EC2 instances?

A. Security groups

B. Elastic network interfaces

C. Network ACLs

D. VPC Flow Logs

322. Which AWS service can be used to automatically scale an application up and down without making capacity planning decisions?

A. Amazon AutoScaling

B. Amazon Redshift

C. AWS CloudTrail

D. AWS Lambda

323. AWS Enterprise Support users have access to which service or feature that is not available to users with other AWS Support plans?

A. AWS Trusted Advisor

B. AWS Support case

C. Concierge team

D. Amazon Connect

324. A company wants to migrate a MySQL database to AWS but does not have the budget for Database Administrators to handle routine tasks including provisioning, patching, and performing backups. Which AWS service will support this use case?

A. Amazon RDS

B. Amazon DynamoDB

C. Amazon DocumentDB

D. Amazon ElastiCache

325. A company wants to expand from one AWS Region into a second AWS Region. What does the company need to do to start supporting the new Region?

   A. Contact an AWS Account Manager to sign a new contract
   B. Move an Availability Zone to the new Region
   C. Begin deploying resources in the second Region
   D. Download the AWS Management Console for the new Region

326. A user must meet compliance and software licensing requirements that state a workload must be hosted on a physical server. Which Amazon EC2 instance pricing option will meet these requirements?

   A. Dedicated Hosts
   B. Dedicated Instances
   C. Spot Instances
   D. Reserved Instances

327. Which AWS service will provide a way to generate encryption keys that can be used to encrypt data? (Choose two.)

   A. Amazon Macie
   B. AWS Certificate Manager
   C. AWS Key Management Service (AWS KMS)
   D. AWS Secrets Manager
   E. AWS CloudHSM

328. A company is planning to migrate from on-premises to the AWS Cloud. Which AWS tool or service provides detailed reports on estimated cost savings after migration?

A. AWS Total Cost of Ownership (TCO) Calculator

B. Cost Explorer

C. AWS Budgets

D. AWS Migration Hub

329. What can assist in evaluating an application for migration to the cloud? (Choose two.)

A. AWS Trusted Advisor

B. AWS Professional Services

C. AWS Systems Manager

D. AWS Partner Network (APN)

E. AWS Secrets Manager

330. Which AWS service helps users meet contractual and regulatory compliance requirements for data security by using dedicated hardware appliances within the AWS Cloud?

A. AWS Secrets Manager

B. AWS CloudHSM

C. AWS Key Management Service (AWS KMS)

D. AWS Directory Service

331. Under the AWS shared responsibility model, the customer manages which of the following? (Choose two.)

   A. Decommissioning of physical storage devices

   B. Security group and ACL configuration

   C. Patch management of an Amazon RDS instance operating system

   D. Controlling physical access to data centers

   E. Patch management of an Amazon EC2 instance operating system

332. Which AWS service is suitable for an event-driven workload?

   A. Amazon EC2

   B. AWS Elastic Beanstalk

   C. AWS Lambda

   D. Amazon Lumberyard

333. What is a value proposition of the AWS Cloud?

   A. AWS is responsible for security in the AWS Cloud

   B. No long-term contract is required

   C. Provision new servers in days

   D. AWS manages user applications in the AWS Cloud

334. What is a characteristic of Amazon S3 cross-region replication?

   A. Both source and destination S3 buckets must have versioning disabled

   B. The source and destination S3 buckets cannot be in different AWS Regions

   C. S3 buckets configured for cross-region replication can be owned by a single AWS account or by different accounts

   D. The source S3 bucket owner must have the source and destination AWS Regions disabled for their account

335. What is a user responsible for when running an application in the AWS Cloud?

A. Managing physical hardware
B. Updating the underlying hypervisor
C. Providing a list of users approved for data center access
D. Managing application software updates

336. A company that does business online needs to quickly deliver new functionality in an iterative manner, minimizing the time to market. Which AWS Cloud feature can provide this?

A. Elasticity
B. High availability
C. Agility
D. Reliability

337. Which features or services can be used to monitor costs and expenses for an AWS account? (Choose two.)

A. AWS Cost and Usage report
B. AWS product pages
C. AWS Simple Monthly Calculator
D. Billing alerts and Amazon CloudWatch alarms
E. AWS Price List API

338. Amazon Route 53 enables users to:

A. encrypt data in transit
B. register DNS domain names
C. generate and manage SSL certificates
D. establish a dedicated network connection to AWS

339. Which AWS service helps identify malicious or unauthorized activities in AWS accounts and workloads?

   A. Amazon Rekognition

   B. AWS Trusted Advisor

   C. Amazon GuardDuty

   D. Amazon CloudWatch

340. A company wants to try a third-party ecommerce solution before deciding to use it long term. Which AWS service or tool will support this effort?

   A. AWS Marketplace

   B. AWS Partner Network (APN)

   C. AWS Managed Services

   D. AWS Service Catalog

341. Which AWS service is a managed NoSQL database?

   A. Amazon Redshift

   B. Amazon DynamoDB

   C. Amazon Aurora

   D. Amazon RDS for MariaDB

342. Which AWS service should be used to create a billing alarm?

   A. AWS Trusted Advisor

   B. AWS CloudTrail

   C. Amazon CloudWatch

   D. Amazon QuickSight

343. A company is hosting a web application in a Docker container on Amazon EC2. AWS is responsible for which of the following tasks?

A. Scaling the web application and services developed with Docker

B. Provisioning or scheduling containers to run on clusters and maintain their availability

C. Performing hardware maintenance in the AWS facilities that run the AWS Cloud

D. Managing the guest operating system, including updates and security patches

344. Users are reporting latency when connecting to a website with a global customer base. Which AWS service will improve the customer experience by reducing latency?

A. Amazon CloudFront

B. AWS Direct Connect

C. Amazon EC2 Auto Scaling

D. AWS Transit Gateway

345. Which actions represent best practices for using AWS IAM? (Choose two.)

A. Configure a strong password policy

B. Share the security credentials among users of AWS accounts who are in the same Region

C. Use access keys to log in to the AWS Management Console

D. Rotate access keys on a regular basis

E. Avoid using IAM roles to delegate permissions

346. Which AWS feature or service can be used to capture information about incoming and outgoing trafic in an AWS VPC infrastructure?

   A. AWS Config
   B. VPC Flow Logs
   C. AWS Trusted Advisor
   D. AWS CloudTrail

347. A company wants to use an AWS service to monitor the health of application endpoints, with the ability to route trafic to healthy regional endpoints to improve application availability. Which service will support these requirements?

   A. Amazon Inspector
   B. Amazon CloudWatch
   C. AWS Global Accelerator
   D. Amazon CloudFront

348. According to the AWS Well-Architected Framework, what change management steps should be taken to achieve reliability in the AWS Cloud? (Choose two.)

   A. Use AWS Config to generate an inventory of AWS resources
   B. Use service limits to prevent users from creating or making changes to AWS resources
   C. Use AWS CloudTrail to record AWS API calls into an auditable log file
   D. Use AWS Certificate Manager to whitelist approved AWS resources and services
   E. Use Amazon GuardDuty to validate configuration changes made to AWS resources

349. Which service can be used to monitor and receive alerts for AWS account root user AWS Management Console sign-in events?

A. Amazon CloudWatch

B. AWS Config

C. AWS Trusted Advisor

D. AWS IAM

350. Which design principle should be considered when architecting in the AWS Cloud?

A. Think of servers as non-disposable resources

B. Use synchronous integration of services

C. Design loosely coupled components

D. Implement the least permissive rules for security groups

351. Which AWS services can be used to move data from on-premises data centers to AWS? (Choose two.)

A. AWS Snowball

B. AWS Lambda

C. Amazon ElastiCache

D. AWS Database Migration Service (AWS DMS)

E. Amazon API Gateway

352. A batch workload takes 5 hours to finish on an Amazon EC2 instance. The amount of data to be processed doubles monthly and the processing time is proportional. What is the best cloud architecture to address this consistently growing demand?

   A. Run the application on a bigger EC2 instance size.

   B. Switch to an EC2 instance family that better matches batch requirements.

   C. Distribute the application across multiple EC2 instances and run the workload in parallel.

   D. Run the application on a bare metal EC2 instance.

353. Each department within a company has its own independent AWS account and its own payment method. New company leadership wants to centralize departmental governance and consolidate payments. How can this be achieved using AWS services or features?

   A. Forward monthly invoices for each account. Then create IAM roles to allow cross-account access.

   B. Create a new AWS account. Then configure AWS Organizations and invite all existing accounts to join.

   C. Configure AWS Organizations in each of the existing accounts. Then link all accounts together.

   D. Use Cost Explorer to combine costs from all accounts. Then replicate IAM policies across accounts.

354. The ability to horizontally scale Amazon EC2 instances based on demand is an example of which concept in the AWS Cloud value proposition?

   A. Economy of scale

   B. Elasticity

   C. High availability

   D. Agility

355. An ecommerce company anticipates a huge increase in web trafic for two very popular upcoming shopping holidays. Which AWS service or feature can be configured to dynamically adjust resources to meet this change in demand?

   A. AWS CloudTrail

   B. Amazon EC2 Auto Scaling

   C. Amazon Forecast

   D. AWS Config

356. Which AWS service enables users to securely connect to AWS resources over the public internet?

   A. Amazon VPC peering

   B. AWS Direct Connect

   C. AWS VPN

   D. Amazon Pinpoint

357. Which tool is used to forecast AWS spending?

   A. AWS Trusted Advisor

   B. AWS Organizations

   C. Cost Explorer

   D. Amazon Inspector

358. A company is running an ecommerce application hosted in Europe. To decrease latency for users who access the website from other parts of the world, the company would like to cache frequently accessed static content closer to the users. Which AWS service will support these requirements?

   A. Amazon ElastiCache

   B. Amazon CloudFront

   C. Amazon Elastic File System (Amazon EFS)

   D. Amazon Elastic Block Store (Amazon EBS)

359. Which of the following is a component of the AWS Global Infrastructure?

   A. Amazon Alexa

   B. AWS Regions

   C. Amazon Lightsail

   D. AWS Organizations

360. Which AWS service will help users determine if an application running on an Amazon EC2 instance has sufficient CPU capacity?

   A. Amazon CloudWatch

   B. AWS Config

   C. AWS CloudTrail

   D. Amazon Inspector

361. Why is it beneficial to use Elastic Load Balancers with applications?

    A. They allow for the conversion from Application Load Balancers to Classic Load Balancers.
    B. They are capable of handling constant changes in network trafic patterns.
    C. They automatically adjust capacity.
    D. They are provided at no charge to users.

362. Which tasks are the customer's responsibility in the AWS shared responsibility model? (Choose two.)

    A. Infrastructure facilities access management
    B. Cloud infrastructure hardware lifecycle management
    C. Configuration management of user›s applications
    D. Networking infrastructure protection
    E. Security groups configuration

363. IT systems should be designed to reduce interdependencies, so that a change or failure in one component does not cascade to other components. This is an example of which principle of cloud architecture design?

    A. Scalability
    B. Loose coupling
    C. Automation
    D. Automatic scaling

364. Which AWS service or feature can enhance network security by blocking requests from a particular network for a web application on AWS? (Choose two.)

   A. AWS WAF

   B. AWS Trusted Advisor

   C. AWS Direct Connect

   D. AWS Organizations

   E. Network ACLs

365. An application runs on multiple Amazon EC2 instances that access a shared file system simultaneously.

   A. Amazon EBS

   B. Amazon EFS

   C. Amazon S3

   D. AWS Artifact

366. A web application is hosted on AWS using an Elastic Load Balancer, multiple Amazon EC2 instances, and Amazon RDS. Which security measures fall under the responsibility of AWS? (Choose two.)

   A. Running a virus scan on EC2 instances

   B. Protecting against IP spoofing and packet snifing

   C. Installing the latest security patches on the RDS instance

   D. Encrypting communication between the EC2 instances and the Elastic Load Balancer

   E. Configuring a security group and a network access control list (NACL) for EC2 instances

367. What is the benefit of elasticity in the AWS Cloud?

   A. Ensure web trafic is automatically spread across multiple AWS Regions.

   B. Minimize storage costs by automatically archiving log data.

   C. Enable AWS to automatically select the most cost-effective services.

   D. Automatically adjust the required compute capacity to maintain consistent performance.

368. The continual reduction of AWS Cloud pricing is due to:

   A. pay-as-you go pricing

   B. the AWS global infrastructure

   C. economies of scale

   D. reserved storage pricing

369. A company needs an Amazon S3 bucket that cannot have any public objects due to compliance requirements. How can this be accomplished?

   A. Enable S3 Block Public Access from the AWS Management Console.

   B. Hold a team meeting to discuss the importance if only uploading private S3 objects.

   C. Require all S3 objects to be manually approved before uploading.

   D. Create a service to monitor all S3 uploads and remove any public uploads.

370. A Cloud Practitioner identifies a billing issue after examining the AWS Cost and Usage report in the AWS Management Console.

    A. Open a detailed case related to billing and submit it to AWS Support for help.
    B. Upload data describing the issue to a new object in a private Amazon S3 bucket.
    C. Create a pricing application and deploy it to a right-sized Amazon EC2 instance for more information.
    D. Proceed with creating a new dashboard in Amazon QuickSight.

371. What does the AWS Simple Monthly Calculator do?

    A. Compares on-premises costs to colocation environments
    B. Estimates monthly billing based on projected usage
    C. Estimates power consumption at existing data centers
    D. Estimates CPU utilization

372. Who is responsible for patching the guest operating system for Amazon RDS?

    A. The AWS Product team
    B. The customer Database Administrator
    C. Managed partners
    D. AWS Support

373. Which AWS services may be scaled using AWS Auto Scaling? (Choose two.)

    A. Amazon EC2
    B. Amazon DynamoDB
    C. Amazon S3
    D. Amazon Route 53
    E. Amazon Redshift

374. Which of the following are benefits of AWS Global Accelerator? (Choose two.)

    A. Reduced cost to run services on AWS
    B. Improved availability of applications deployed on AWS
    C. Higher durability of data stored on AWS
    D. Decreased latency to reach applications deployed on AWS
    E. Higher security of data stored on AWS

375. A user who wants to get help with billing and reactivate a suspended account should submit an account and billing request to:

    A. the AWS Support forum
    B. AWS Abuse
    C. an AWS Solutions Architect
    D. AWS Support

376. Which AWS Cloud best practice uses the elasticity and agility of cloud computing?

    A. Provision capacity based on past usage and theoretical peaks
    B. Dynamically and predictively scale to meet usage demands
    C. Build the application and infrastructure in a data center that grants physical access
    D. Break apart the application into loosely coupled components

377. Which method helps to optimize costs of users moving to the AWS Cloud?

   A. Paying only for what is used
   B. Purchasing hardware before it is needed
   C. Manually provisioning cloud resources
   D. Purchasing for the maximum possible load

378. Under the AWS shared responsibility model, which of the following is a customer responsibility?

   A. Installing security patches for the Xen and KVM hypervisors
   B. Installing operating system patches for Amazon DynamoDB
   C. Installing operating system security patches for Amazon EC2 database instances
   D. Installing operating system security patches for Amazon RDS database instances

379. The AWS Cost Management tools give users the ability to do which of the following? (Choose two.)

   A. Terminate all AWS resources automatically if budget thresholds are exceeded.
   B. Break down AWS costs by day, service, and linked AWS account.
   C. Create budgets and receive notifications if current of forecasted usage exceeds the budgets.
   D. Switch automatically to Reserved Instances or Spot Instances, whichever is most cost-effective.
   E. Move data stored in Amazon S3 to a more cost-effective storage class.

380. Under the AWS shared responsibility model, the security and patching of the guest operating system is the responsibility of:

A. AWS Support
B. the customer
C. AWS Systems Manager
D. AWS Config

381. Which AWS service makes it easy to create and manage AWS users and groups, and provide them with secure access to AWS resources at no charge?

A. AWS Direct Connect
B. Amazon Connect
C. AWS Identity and Access Management (IAM)
D. AWS Firewall Manager

382. Which AWS service provides on-demand of AWS security and compliance documentation?

A. AWS Directory Service
B. AWS Artifact
C. AWS Trusted Advisor
D. Amazon Inspector

383. Which AWS service can be used to turn text into life-like speech?

A. Amazon Polly
B. Amazon Transcribe
C. Amazon Rekognition
D. Amazon Lex

384. What is one of the core principles to follow when designing a highly available application in the AWS Cloud?

  A. Design using a serverless architecture

  B. Assume that all components within an application can fail

  C. Design AWS Auto Scaling into every application

  D. Design all components using open-source code

385. A user needs to generate a report that outlines the status of key security checks in an AWS account. The report must include: The status of Amazon S3 bucket permissions. Whether multi-factor authentication is enabled for the AWS account root user. If any security groups are configured to allow unrestricted access. Where can all this information be found in one location?

  A. Amazon QuickSight dashboard

  B. AWS CloudTrail trails

  C. AWS Trusted Advisor report

  D. IAM credential report

386. Which Amazon EC2 pricing model should be used to comply with per-core software license requirements?

  A. Dedicated Hosts

  B. On-Demand Instances

  C. Spot Instances

  D. Reserved Instances

387. Which of the AWS global infrastructure is used to cache copies of content for faster delivery to users across the globe?

A. AWS Regions

B. Availability Zones

C. Edge locations

D. Data centers

388. Using AWS Config to record, audit, and evaluate changes to AWS resources to enable traceability is an example of which AWS Well-Architected

A. Security

B. Operational excellence

C. Performance eficiency

D. Cost optimization

389. A user needs to quickly deploy a non-relational database on AWS. The user does not want to manage the underlying hardware or the database software. Which AWS service can be used to accomplish this?

A. Amazon RDS

B. Amazon DynamoDB

C. Amazon Aurora

D. Amazon Redshift

390. A Cloud Practitioner is developing a disaster recovery plan and intends to replicate data between multiple geographic areas. Which of the following meets these requirements?

A. AWS Accounts

B. AWS Regions

C. Availability Zones

D. Edge locations

391. Which features and benefits does the AWS Organizations service provide? (Choose two.)

   A. Establishing real-time communications between members of an internal team
   B. Facilitating the use of NoSQL databases
   C. Providing automated security checks
   D. Implementing consolidated billing
   E. Enforcing the governance of AWS accounts

392. Which AWS service is used to automate configuration management using Chef and Puppet?

   A. AWS Config
   B. AWS OpsWorks
   C. AWS CloudFormation
   D. AWS Systems Manager

393. Which tool is best suited for combining the billing of AWS accounts that were previously independent from one another?

   A. Detailed billing report
   B. Consolidated billing
   C. AWS Cost and Usage report
   D. Cost allocation report

394. The AWS Total Cost of Ownership (TCO) Calculator is used to:

   A. receive reports that break down AWS Cloud compute costs by duration, resource, or tags

   B. estimate savings when comparing the AWS Cloud to an on-premises environment

   C. estimate a monthly bill for the AWS Cloud resources that will be used

   D. enable billing alerts to monitor actual AWS costs compared to estimated costs

395. Which AWS services can be used to provide network connectivity between an on-premises network and a VPC? (Choose two.)

   A. Amazon Route 53
   B. AWS Direct Connect
   C. AWS Data Pipeline
   D. AWS VPN
   E. Amazon Connect

396. Under the AWS shared responsibility model, which of the following are customer responsibilities? (Choose two.)

   A. Setting up server-side encryption on an Amazon S3 bucket

   B. Amazon RDS instance patching
   C. Network and firewall configurations
   D. Physical security of data center facilities
   E. Compute capacity availability

397. What is the MINIMUM AWS Support plan level that will provide users with access to the AWS Support API?

A. Developer

B. Enterprise

C. Business

D. Basic

398. A company has deployed several relational databases on Amazon EC2 instances. Every month, the database software vendor releases new security patches that need to be applied to the databases. What is the MOST eficient way to apply the security patches?

A. Connect to each database instance on a monthly basis, and download and apply the necessary security patches from the vendor.

B. Enable automatic patching for the instances using the Amazon RDS console.

C. In AWS Config, configure a rule for the instances and the required patch level.

D. Use AWS Systems Manager to automate database patching according to a schedule.

399. A company wants to use Amazon Elastic Compute Cloud (Amazon EC2) to deploy a global commercial application. The deployment solution should be built with the highest redundancy and fault tolerance. Based on this situation, the Amazon EC2 instances should be deployed:

A. in a single Availability Zone in one AWS Region

B. with multiple Elastic Network Interfaces belonging to different subnets

C. across multiple Availability Zones in one AWS Region

D. across multiple Availability Zones in two AWS Regions

400. A company has an application with users in both Australia and Brazil. All the company infrastructure is currently provisioned in the Asia Pacific (Sydney) Region in Australia, and Brazilian users are experiencing high latency. What should the company do to reduce latency?

A. Implement AWS Direct Connect for users in Brazil

B. Provision resources in the South America (São Paulo) Region in Brazil

C. Use AWS Transit Gateway to quickly route users from Brazil to the application

D. Launch additional Amazon EC2 instances in Sydney to handle the demand

SOLUTIONS

1. **Correct Answer:** *C*

   Reference:
   https://www.whizlabs.com/blog/aws-security-shared-responsibility/

2. **Correct Answer:** *C*

   Reference:
   https://aws.amazon.com/blogs/startups/how-to-set-aws-budget-when-paying-with-aws-credits/

3. **Correct Answer:** *C*

   Reference:
   https://aws.amazon.com/blogs/startups/how-to-set-aws-budget-when-paying-with-aws-credits/

4. **Correct Answer:** *C*

   Reference:
   https://aws.amazon.com/blogs/startups/how-to-set-aws-budget-when-paying-with-aws-credits/

5. **Correct Answer:** *C*

6. **Correct Answer:** *C*

7. **Correct Answer:** *AB*

   Reference: https://aws.amazon.com/sql/

8. **Correct Answer:** *B*

9. **Correct Answer:** *C*

   Reference: https://aws.amazon.com/ec2/pricing/

10. **Correct Answer:** *CD*

11. **Correct Answer:** *B*

   Reference: https://aws.amazon.com/cloudtrail/

12. **Correct Answer:** *BE*

13. **Correct Answer:** *AB*

   Reference: https://www.stratoscale.com/blog/cloud/building-hybrid-cloud-environment-using-amazon-cloud/

14. **Correct Answer:** *C*

15. **Correct Answer:** *D*

16. Correct Answer: B

   Reference: https://aws.amazon.com/about-aws/global-infrastructure/regions_az/#Region_Maps_and_Edge_Networks

17. **Correct Answer:** *BCD*

18. **Correct Answer:** *AD*

   Reference: https://docs.aws.amazon.com/awsaccountbilling/latest/aboutv2/consolidated-billing.html

19. **Correct Answer:** *C*

   Reference: https://aws.amazon.com/ec2/pricing/reserved-instances/pricing/

20. **Correct Answer:** *D*

    Reference:
    https://d1.awsstatic.com/whitepapers/introduction-to-aws-cloud-economics- final.pdf(10)

21. **Correct Answer:** *C*

    Reference: https://www.edureka.co/community/600/what-is-an-edge-location-in-aws

22. **Correct Answer:** *C*

    Reference:
    https://aws.amazon.com/blogs/security/how-to-restrict-amazon-s3-bucket-access-to-a-specific-iam-role/

23. **Correct Answer:** *C*

24. **Correct Answer:** *C*

    Reference:
    https://aws.amazon.com/ec2/pricing/reserved-instances/

25. **Correct Answer:** *C*

26. **Correct Answer:** *B*

    Reference: https://aws.amazon.com/elasticloadbalancing/

27. **Correct Answer:** *C*

    Reference: https://aws.amazon.com/compliance/soc-faqs/

28. **Correct Answer:** *BD*

    Reference:
    https://aws.amazon.com/compliance/shared-responsibility-model/

29. **Correct Answer:** *C*

30. **Correct Answer:** *B*

    Reference: https://d1.awsstatic.com/whitepapers/AWS_ Cloud_Best_Practices.pdf

31. **Correct Answer:** *DE*

32. **Correct Answer:** *BE*

33. **Correct Answer:** *A*

34. **Correct Answer:** *A*

    Reference: https://aws.amazon.com/rds/aurora/serverless/

35. **Correct Answer:** *A*

    Reference: https://docs.aws.amazon.com/whitepapers/latest/aws-overview/global-infrastructure.html

36. **Correct Answer:** *D*

    Reference: https://aws.amazon.com/compliance/shared-responsibility-model/

37. **Correct Answer:** *B*

38. **Correct Answer:** *C*

39. **Correct Answer:** *A*

40. **Correct Answer:** *B*

Reference:
https://docs.aws.amazon.com/IAM/latest/UserGuide/id_credentials_access-keys.html

41. **Correct Answer:** *C*

Reference: https://aws.amazon.com/dynamodb/

42. **Correct Answer:** *D*

Reference:
https://aws.amazon.com/blogs/enterprise-strategy/risk-is-lack-of-agility/

43. **Correct Answer:** *B*

Reference: https://aws.amazon.com/organizations/

44. **Correct Answer:** *A*

Reference: https://aws.amazon.com/solutions/case-studies/encoding/

45. **Correct Answer:** *B*

46. **Correct Answer:** *B*

47. **Correct Answer:** *C*

Reference: https://aws.amazon.com/compliance/shared-responsibility-model/

48. **Correct Answer:** *C*

Reference: https://aws.amazon.com/answers/account-management/aws-multi-account-billing-strategy/

49. **Correct Answer:** *DE*

50. **Correct Answer:** *A*

Reference:
https://aws.amazon.com/getting-started/tutorials/get-a-domain/

51. **Correct Answer:** *AC*

52. **Correct Answer:** *D*

Reference: https://aws.amazon.com/getting-started/projects/host-static-website/

53. **Correct Answer:** *D*

Reference: https://aws.amazon.com/ec2/spot/

54. **Correct Answer:** *B*

55. **Correct Answer:** *A*

56. **Correct Answer:** *D*

Reference: https://aws.amazon.com/redshift/

57. **Correct Answer:** *B*

Reference: https://aws.amazon.com/elasticloadbalancing/

58. **Correct Answer:** *AC*

59. Correct Answer: B

60. **Correct Answer:** *BE*

    Reference:
    https://aws.amazon.com/getting-started/tutorials/deliver-content-faster/ https://aws.amazon.com/cloudfront/

61. **Correct Answer:** *C*

    Reference: https://aws.amazon.com/enterprise/hybrid/

62. **Correct Answer:** *C*

63. **Correct Answer:** *D*

    Reference:
    https://aws.amazon.com/what-is-cloud-object-storage/

64. **Correct Answer:** *B*

    Reference:
     https://docs.aws.amazon.com/IAM/latest/UserGuide/id_credentials_access-keys.html

65. **Correct Answer:** *BC*

    Reference: https://aws.amazon.com/security/

66. **Correct Answer:** *D*

    Amazon Relational Database Service (Amazon RDS) makes it easy to set up, operate, and scale a relational database in the cloud. It provides cost-eficient and resizable capacity while automating time-consuming administration tasks such as hardware provisioning, database setup, patching and backups. It frees you to focus on your applications so you can give them the fast performance, high availability, security and compatibility they need.

    Reference: https://aws.amazon.com/rds/?c=db&sec=srv

67. **Correct Answer:** *D*

Amazon Elastic File System (Amazon EFS) provides a simple, scalable, fully managed elastic NFS file system for use with AWS Cloud services and on-premises resources. It is built to scale on demand to petabytes without disrupting applications, growing and shrinking automatically as you add and remove files, eliminating the need to provision and manage capacity to accommodate growth. Amazon EFS is designed to provide the throughput, IOPS, and low latency needed for Linux workloads. Throughput and IOPS scale as a file system grows and can burst to higher throughput levels for short periods of time to support the unpredictable performance needs of file workloads. For the most demanding workloads, Amazon EFS can support performance over 10 GB/sec and up to 500,000 IOPS.

68. **Correct Answer:** *D*

Cloud services main proposition is to provide elasticity through horizontal scaling. It›s already there. As for using largest instance possible, it is not a design principle that helps cloud applications in anyway. Scrum development process is not related to architecting. Therefore, a key principle is to provision your application for on-demand capacity. Peak loads is something that cloud applications experience everyday. Peak load management should be a necessary part of cloud application design principle.

Reference: https://d1.awsstatic.com/whitepapers/AWS_Cloud_Best_Practices.pdf

69. **Correct Answer:** *B*

Explanation -

Amazon S3 Glacier is a secure, durable, and low-cost storage class of S3 for data archiving and long-term backup. Customers can store large or small amounts of data for as little as

$0.004 per gigabyte per month. The S3 Glacier storage class is ideal for archives where data is regularly retrieved and some of the data may be needed in minutes.

Amazon RDS is a relational database service that hosts databases. It helps you create and manage databases. Amazon Snowball is a petabyte- scale data transfer service that provides cost eficient data transfer to AWS from tamper proof physical devices. Similarly, Elastic block storage offers persistent block storage volumes for EC2 instances.

Reference:
https://aws.amazon.com/backup-restore/services/

70. **Correct Answer:** *B*

71. **Correct Answer:** *D*

AWS Direct Connect enables you to securely connect your AWS environment to your on-premises data center or ofice location over a standard 1 gigabit or 10 gigabit Ethernet fiber-optic connection. AWS Direct Connect offers dedicated high speed, low latency connection, which bypasses internet service providers in your network path. An AWS Direct Connect location provides access to Amazon Web Services in the region it is associated with, as well as access to other US regions. AWS Direct Connect allows you to logically partition the fiber-optic connections into multiple logical connections called Virtual Local Area Networks (VLAN). You can take advantage of these logical connections to improve security, differentiate trafic, and achieve compliance requirements. Reference: https://aws.amazon.com/getting-started/projects/connect-data-center-to-aws/

72. **Correct Answer:** *B*

AWS Lambda is an integral part of coding on AWS. It reduces physical compute footprint by utilizing aws cloud services to run code.

73. **Correct Answer:** *A*

AWS Personal Health Dashboard provides alerts and remediation guidance when AWS is experiencing events that may impact you. While the Service Health

Dashboard displays the general status of AWS services, Personal Health Dashboard gives you a personalized view into the performance and availability of the AWS services underlying your AWS resources. Reference: https://aws.amazon.com/premiumsupport/technology/personal-health-dashboard/

74. **Correct Answer:** *AD*

Like your customized cloud expert, AWS Trusted Advisor analyzes your AWS environment and provides best practice recommendations in five categories: cost optimization, performance, security, fault tolerance and service limits.

Reference: https://aws.amazon.com/premiumsupport/technology/trusted-advisor/

75. Correct Answer: C AWS Compliance enables customers to establish and operate in an AWS security control environment

- The shared responsibility model is part of AWS Compliance program
- The Security of the cloud is managed by Amazon AWS provider
- The Security in the cloud is responsibility of the customer
- The customer is responsible for their information and data, their secure transmission, integrity, and encryption

- Also, the customer is responsible for managing, support, patching and control of the guest operating system and AWS services provided like EC2
- AWS customers retain control and ownership of their data
- The AWS network provides significant protection against traditional network security issues and the customer can implement further protection

Reference: https://www.whizlabs.com/blog/aws-security-shared-responsibility/

76. **Correct Answer: A**

AWS Marketplace is a digital catalog with thousands of software listings from independent software vendors that make it easy to find, test, buy, and deploy software that runs on AWS.

Reference:https://aws.amazon.com

77. **Correct Answer:** B

Developer and IT staff productivity accounted for nearly 30% of overall financial benefits. The remaining benefits were driven by the flexibility and agility of

Amazon cloud infrastructure services, which make it easier to trial new business models, support revenue-generating applications, and provide more reliable services to end users.

Reference:

https://media.amazonwebservices.com/IDC_Business_Value_of_AWS_Accelerates_Over_time.pdf

78. **Correct Answer:** *A*

Use Dedicated Hosts to launch Amazon EC2 instances on physical servers that are dedicated for your use. Dedicated Hosts give you additional visibility and control over how instances are placed on a physical server, and you can reliably use the same physical server over time. As a result, Dedicated Hosts enable you to use your existing server-bound software licenses like Windows Server and address corporate compliance and regulatory requirements.

79. **Correct Answer:** *D*

AWS CloudFormation provides a common language for you to describe and provision all the infrastructure resources in your cloud environment. CloudFormation allows you to use a simple text file to model and provision, in an automated and secure manner, all the resources needed for your applications across all regions and accounts. This file serves as the single source of truth for your cloud environment.

Reference:https://aws.amazon.com/cloudformation/

80. **Correct Answer:** *A*

AWS Config is a service that enables you to assess, audit, and evaluate the configurations of your AWS resources. Config continuously monitors and records your

AWS resource configurations and allows you to automate the evaluation of recorded configurations against desired configurations. With Config, you can review changes in configurations and relationships between AWS resources, dive into detailed resource configuration histories, and determine your overall compliance against the configurations specified in your internal guidelines. This enables you to simplify compliance auditing, security analysis, change management, and operational troubleshooting.

Reference:https://aws.amazon.com/config/

81. **Correct Answer:** *B*

Amazon CloudWatch is basically a metrics repository. An AWS service's such as Amazon EC2 puts metrics into the repository, and you retrieve statistics based on those metrics. If you put your own custom metrics into the repository, you can retrieve statistics on these metrics as well.

Reference:
https://docs.aws.amazon.com/AmazonCloudWatch/latest/monitoring/cloudwatch_architecture.html

82. **Correct Answer:** *B*

use the consolidated billing feature in AWS Organizations to consolidate billing and payment for multiple AWS accounts or multiple Amazon Internet Services Pvt. Ltd (AISPL) accounts. Every organization in AWS Organizations has a master account that pays the charges of all the member accounts.

83. **Correct Answer:** *BC*

Reference: https://docs.aws.amazon.com/codedeploy/latest/userguide/instances-on-premises.html https://aws.amazon.com/blogs/aws/opsworks-on- prem-and-existing-instances/

84. **Correct Answer:** *C*

In the new model, the Spot prices are more predictable, updated less frequently, and are determined by supply and demand for Amazon EC2 spare capacity, not bid prices.

Reference:
https://aws.amazon.com/blogs/compute/new-amazon-ec2-spot-pricing/

85. **Correct Answer:** *CE*

Rearchitecting applications involves sweeping change where an old monolithic application is completely revamped according to modern microservices architecture. Using individual components to re-architect a big application is one part of the process. The most important part is to design the application for scalability because the level of investment for a monolithic application can only be justified when resilience and scalability is needed.

Reference:
https://www.architech.ca/re-architect-applications/

86. **Correct Answer:** *B*

Reference: https://aws.amazon.com/premiumsupport/plans/

87. **Correct Answer:** *A*

WS Artifact is your go-to, central resource for compliance-related information that matters to you. It provides on-demand access to AWS›s security and compliance reports and select online agreements. The AWS SOC 2 report is particularly helpful for completing questionnaires because it provides a comprehensive description of the implementation and operating effectiveness of AWS security controls. Another useful document is the Executive Briefing within the AWS

FedRAMP Partner Package. Reference: https://aws.amazon.com/compliance/faq/

88. **Correct Answer:** *C*

Personal Health Dashboard gives you a personalized view of the status of the AWS services that power your applications, enabling you to quickly see when AWS is experiencing issues that may impact you. For example, in the event of a lost EBS volume associated with one of your EC2 instances, you would gain quick visibility into the status of the specific service you are using, helping save precious time troubleshooting to determine root cause.

Reference:https://aws.amazon.com/premiumsupport/technology/personal-health-dashboard/

89. **Correct Answer:** *A*

If you have multiple standalone accounts, your charges might decrease if you add the accounts to an organization. AWS combines usage from all accounts in the organization to qualify you for volume pricing discounts.

Reference:
https://help.nops.io/consolidated-billing

90. **Correct Answer:** *D*

AWS customers are welcome to carry out security assessments or penetration tests against their AWS infrastructure without prior approval for 8 services.

Reference:
https://aws.amazon.com/security/penetration-testing/

91. **Correct Answer:** *B*

To use Amazon EC2, you simply:

- Select a pre-configured, templated Amazon Machine Image (AMI) to get up and running immediately. Or create an AMI containing your applications, libraries, data, and associated configuration settings.

- Configure security and network access on your Amazon EC2 instance.

- Choose which instance type(s) you want, then start, terminate, and monitor as many instances of your AMI as needed, using the web service APIs or the variety of management tools provided.

- Determine whether you want to run in multiple locations, utilize static IP endpoints, or attach persistent block storage to your instances.

- Pay only for the resources that you actually consume, like instance-hours or data transfer. Reference: https://aws. amazon.com/ec2/features

92. **Correct Answer:** *A*

Instead of defining permissions for individual IAM users, it's usually more convenient to create groups that relate to job functions (administrators, developers, accounting, etc.). Next, define the relevant permissions for each group. Finally, assign IAM users to those groups. All the users in an IAM group inherit the permissions *assigned* to the group. That way, you can make changes for everyone in a group in just one place. As people move around in your company, you can simply change what IAM group their IAM user belongs to.

Reference: https://docs.aws.amazon.com/IAM/latest/ UserGuide/best-practices.html

93. **Correct Answer:** *D*

AWS Auto Scaling monitors your applications and automatically adjusts capacity to maintain steady, predictable performance at the lowest possible cost. Using

AWS Auto Scaling, it›s easy to setup application scaling for multiple resources across multiple services in minutes. The service provides a simple, powerful user interface that lets you build scaling plans for resources including Amazon EC2 instances and Spot Fleets, Amazon ECS tasks, Amazon DynamoDB tables and indexes, and Amazon Aurora Replicas. AWS Auto Scaling makes scaling simple with recommendations that allow you to optimize performance, costs, or balance between them. If you›re already using Amazon EC2 Auto Scaling to dynamically scale your Amazon EC2 instances, you can now combine it with AWS Auto

Scaling to scale additional resources for other AWS services. With AWS Auto Scaling, your applications always have the right resources at the right time.

Reference: https://aws.amazon.com/autoscaling/

94. **Correct Answer:** *AD*

Reference:http://jayendrapatil.com/aws-global-vs-regional-vs-az-resources/

95. Correct Answer: A AWS Artifact is your go-to, central resource for compliance-related information that matters to you. It provides on-demand access to AWS security and compliance reports and select online agreements. Reports available in AWS Artifact include our Service Organization Control (SOC) reports, Payment Card Industry (PCI) reports, and certifications from accreditation bodies across geographies and compliance verticals that validate the implementation and operating

effectiveness of AWS security controls. Agreements available in AWS Artifact include the Business Associate Addendum (BAA) and the Nondisclosure Agreement (NDA). Reference: https://aws.amazon.com/artifact/

96. **Correct Answer:** *AC*

97. **Correct Answer:** *C*

98. **Correct Answer:** *D*

99. **Correct Answer:** *AC*

100. **Correct Answer:** *C*

The Cost & Usage Report is your one-stop-shop for accessing the most granular data about your AWS costs and usage. You can also load your cost and usage information into Amazon Athena, Amazon Redshift, AWS QuickSight, or a tool of your choice.

Reference:

https://aws.amazon.com/aws-cost-management/

101. **Correct Answer:** *E*

102. **Correct Answer:** *B*

Loose coupling between services can also be done through asynchronous integration. It involves one component that generates events and another that consumes them. The two components do not integrate through direct point-to-point interaction, but usually through an intermediate durable storage layer. This approach decouples the two components and introduces additional resiliency. So, for example, if a process that is reading messages from the queue fails, messages can still be added to the queue to be processed when the system recovers.

Reference:
https://www.botmetric.com/blog/aws-cloud-architecture-design-principles/

103. **Correct Answer:** *BE*

If you decided to create service accounts (that is, accounts used for programmatic access by applications running outside of the AWS environment) and generate access keys for them, you should create a dedicated service account for each use case. This will allow you to restrict the associated policy to only the permissions needed for the particular use case, limiting the blast radius if the credentials are compromised. For example, if a monitoring tool and a release management tool both require access to your AWS environment, create two separate service accounts with two separate policies that define the minimum set of permissions for each tool.

Reference:
https://aws.amazon.com/blogs/security/guidelines-for-protecting-your-aws-account-while-using-programmatic-access/

104. Correct Answer: C AWS Storage Gateway is a hybrid cloud storage service that gives you on-premises access to virtually unlimited cloud storage. Customers use Storage Gateway to simplify storage management and reduce costs for key hybrid cloud storage use cases. These include moving tape backups to the cloud, reducing on-premises storage with cloud-backed file shares, providing low latency access to data in AWS for on-premises applications, as well as various migration, archiving, processing, and disaster recovery

use cases. Reference: https://aws.amazon.com/storagegate-way/?whats-new-cards.sort-by=item.additionalFields.post-DateTime&whats-new-cards.sort-order=desc

105. **Correct Answer:** *B*

The customer is responsible for managing, support, patching and control of the guest operating system and AWS services provided like EC2.

Reference:
https://www.whizlabs.com/blog/aws-security-shared-responsibility/

106. **Correct Answer:** *A*

Data Center resilience is practiced through Availability Zones across data centers that reduce the impact of failures. Fault isolation improvement can be made to traditional horizontal scaling by sharding (a method of grouping instances into groups called shards, instead of sending the trafic from all users to every node like in the traditional IT structure.)

Reference:
https://www.botmetric.com/blog/aws-cloud-architecture-design-principles/

107. **Correct Answer:** *B*

The enterprise support plans supports technical account manager. Developer and business support plans are devoid of this facility.

Reference:
https://aws.amazon.com/premiumsupport/plans/

108. **Correct Answer:** *B*

109. **Correct Answer:** *C*

Amazon ElastiCache for Redis is a great choice for imple-menting a highly available, distributed, and secure in-mem-ory cache to decrease   access latency, increase throughput, and ease the load off your relational or NoSQL databases and applications. ElastiCache can serve frequently requested items at sub- millisecond response times, and enables you to easily scale for higher loads without growing the costlier backend databases. Database query results caching, per-sistent session caching, and full-page caching are all popular examples of caching with ElastiCache for Redis.

110. **Correct Answer:** *D*

Of course, Amazon is responsible for auditing physical data center assets and resources since it is the property of Ama-zon Inc. Customers have no access to physical sites, hence they are not responsible for maintaining physical data center assets.

111. **Correct Answer:** *BE*

112. **Correct Answer:** CD

Amazon Virtual Private Cloud (Amazon VPC) lets you pro-vision a logically isolated section of the AWS Cloud where you can launch AWS resources in a virtual network that you define. You have complete control over your virtual network-ing environment, including selection of your own IP address range, creation of subnets, and configuration of route tables and network gateways. You can use both IPv4 and IPv6 in your VPC for secure and easy access to resources and appli-cations. You can easily customize the network configuration for your Amazon VPC. For example, you can create a pub-lic-facing subnet for your web servers that has access to the

Internet, and place your backend systems such as databases or application servers in a private-facing subnet with no Internet access. You can leverage multiple layers of security, including security groups and network access control lists, to help control access to Amazon EC2 instances in each subnet. Reference: https://aws.amazon.com/vpc/

113. **Correct Answer:** C

Reference:
https://docs.aws.amazon.com/awsaccountbilling/latest/aboutv2/consolidated-billing.html

114. **Correct Answer:** *A*

115. **Correct Answer:** *CE*

AWS offers a solution that uses AWS CloudTrail to log account activity, Amazon Kinesis to compute and stream metrics in real-time, and Amazon DynamoDB to durably store the computed data. Metrics are calculated for create, modify, and delete API calls for more than 60 supported AWS services. The solution also features a dashboard that visualizes your account activity in real-time.

Reference:
https://aws.amazon.com/solutions/real-time-insights-account-activity/

116. **Correct Answer:** *AC*

117. **Correct Answer:** *D*

Reference:

https://docs.aws.amazon.com/whitepapers/latest/cost-optimization-leveraging-ec2-spot-instances/spot-instance-interruptions.html

118. **Correct Answer:** *B*

This is to achieve High Availability for any web application (in this case SwiftCode) deployed in AWS. The following features will be present:

- High availability across multiple instances/multiple availability zones.
- Auto Scaling of instances (scale up and scale down) based on number of requests coming in
- Additional Security to the instances/database that are in production
- No impact to end users during newer version of code deployment
- No Impact during patching the instances

Reference:
https://betsol.com/2018/01/how-to-make-high-availability-web-applications-on-amazon-web-services/

119. **Correct Answer:** *A*

120. **Correct Answer: A**

You can host a static website on Amazon Simple Storage Service (Amazon S3). On a static website, individual webpages include static content. They might also contain client-side scripts. By contrast, a dynamic website relies on server-side processing, including server-side scripts such as PHP, JSP, or ASP.NET. Amazon S3 does not support server-side scripting. Reference: https://docs.aws.amazon.com/AmazonS3/latest/dev/WebsiteHosting.html

121. **Correct Answer:** *C*

122. **Correct Answer:** *BD*

CloudFront delivers your content through a worldwide network of data centers called edge locations. When a user requests content that you're serving with

CloudFront, the user is routed to the edge location that provides the lowest latency (time delay), so that content is delivered with the best possible performance.

Reference:

https://docs.aws.amazon.com/AmazonCloudFront/latest/DeveloperGuide/Introduction.html

123. **Correct Answer:** *C*

To allow users to perform S3 actions on the bucket from the VPC endpoints or IP addresses, you must explicitly grant those user-level permissions. You can grant user-level permissions on either an AWS Identity and Access Management (IAM) policy or another statement in the bucket policy.

Reference:

https://aws.amazon.com/premiumsupport/knowledge-center/block-s3-trafic-vpc-ip/

124. **Correct Answer:** *B*

Reference:

https://d1.awsstatic.com/whitepapers/AWS_Cloud_Best_Practices.pdf

125. **Correct Answer:** *C*

126. **Correct Answer:** *C*

You can use Cost explorer which is part of Cost and Usage report to forecast future costs of running an application.

Reference:
https://docs.aws.amazon.com/awsaccountbilling/latest/aboutv2/ce-forecast.html

127. **Correct Answer:** *B*

Reference: https://aws.amazon.com/premiumsupport/plans/

128. **Correct Answer:** *C*

In EC2, the AWS IaaS offering, everything from the hypervisor layer down is AWS›s responsibility. A customers poorly coded applications, misconfigured operating systems, or insecure firewall settings will not affect the hypervisor, it will only affect the customers virtual   machines running on that hypervisor.

Reference:
https://www.mindpointgroup.com/blog/the-aws-shared-responsibility-model-part-1-security-in-the-cloud/

129. **Correct Answer:** *C*

On-Demand Capacity Reservations are priced exactly the same as their equivalent (On-Demand) instance usage. If a Capacity Reservation is fully utilized, you only pay for instance usage and nothing towards the Capacity Reservation. If a Capacity Reservation is partially utilized, you pay for the instance usage and for the unused portion of the Capacity Reservation.

Reference:
https://aws.amazon.com/ec2/pricing/on-demand/

130. **Correct Answer:** *D*

Quick Starts are built by AWS solutions architects and partners to help you deploy popular technologies on AWS, based on AWS best practices for security and high availability. These accelerators reduce hundreds of manual procedures into just a few steps, so you can build your production environment quickly and start using it immediately.

Reference:
https://aws.amazon.com/quickstart/?quickstart-all.sort-by=item.additionalFields.updateDate&quickstart-all.sort-order=desc

131. **Correct Answer:** *C*

AWS provides a set of fully managed services that you can use to build and run serverless applications. Serverless applications don›t require provisioning, maintaining, and administering servers for backend components such as compute, databases, storage, stream processing, message queueing, and more. You also no longer need to worry about ensuring application fault tolerance and availability. Instead, AWS handles all of these capabilities for you. Serverless platform includes: AWS lambda, Amazon S3, DynamoDB, API gateway, Amazon SNS, AWS step functions, Amazon kinesis and developing tools and services.

Reference:
https://aws.amazon.com/serverless/

132. **Correct Answer:** *C*

AWS provides a set of fully managed services that you can use to build and run serverless applications. Serverless applications don›t require provisioning, maintaining, and administering servers for backend components such as compute, databases, storage, stream processing, message queueing, and more. You also no longer need to worry about ensuring application fault tolerance and availability. Instead, AWS handles all of these capabilities for you. Serverless platform includes: AWS lambda, Amazon S3, DynamoDB, API gateway, Amazon SNS, AWS step functions, Amazon kinesis and developing tools and services.

Reference:

https://aws.amazon.com/serverless/

133. **Correct Answer:** *B*

Client-side data, application security is the sole responsibility of the customer. Patch management is a shared responsibility. That leaves us with edge location management and since this out of the control of the customer, AWS is the one responsible for it.

Reference:

https://aws.amazon.com/compliance/shared-responsibility-model/

134. **Correct Answer:** *B*

An IAM group is a collection of IAM users. You can use groups to specify permissions for a collection of users, which can make those permissions easier to manage for those users. For example, you could have a group called Admins and give that group the types of permissions that administrators typically need.

Reference:

https://docs.aws.amazon.com/IAM/latest/UserGuide/id.html

135. **Correct Answer:** *BC*

The most celebrated benefit of AWS cloud is elasticity since you can expand the services when you experience more trafic.

Agile developments in AWS Cloud through strategies are day by day becoming more established within the enterprises across the world. With so much improvement and call for optimization in the cloud, it is necessary that these strategies get established from the ground up within the organizations. It is highly important as already enterprises have a lot of bequest, politics and hierarchies which act as barriers in their businesses.

Reference:

https://www.botmetric.com/blog/evolution-agile-enterprises-aws-cloud/

136. **Correct Answer:** *B*

Single sign-on only works when used on a computer that is joined to the AWS Directory Service directory. It cannot be used on computers that are not joined to the directory.

Reference:

https://docs.aws.amazon.com/directoryservice/latest/admin-guide/ms_ad_single_sign_on.html

137. **Correct Answer:** *D*

Each Region is completely independent. Each Availability Zone is isolated, but the Availability Zones in a Region are connected through low- latency links. A Local

Zone is an AWS infrastructure deployment that places select services closer to your end users. A Local Zone is an extension of a Region that is in a different location from your Region. It provides a high-bandwidth backbone to the AWS infrastructure and is ideal for latency-sensitive applications, for example machine learning.

Reference:
https://docs.aws.amazon.com/AWSEC2/latest/UserGuide/using-regions-availability-zones.html

138. **Correct Answer:** *BC*

Reference:
https://d0.awsstatic.com/whitepapers/compliance/AWS_Risk_and_Compliance_Whitepaper.pdf

139. **Correct Answer:** *B*

AWS Artifact is your go-to, central resource for compliance-related information that matters to you. It provides on-demand access to AWS security and compliance reports and select online agreements. Reports available in AWS Artifact include our Service Organization Control (SOC) reports, Payment Card

Industry (PCI) reports, and certifications from accreditation bodies across geographies and compliance verticals that validate the implementation and operating effectiveness of AWS security controls. Agreements available in AWS Artifact include the Business Associate Addendum (BAA) and the Nondisclosure Agreement (NDA).

Reference: https://aws.amazon.com/artifact/

140. **Correct Answer:** *A*

Reference:
https://aws.amazon.com/compliance/shared-responsibility-model/

141. **Correct Answer:** *CD*

Reference:
https://aws.amazon.com/blogs/aws/the-new-aws-tco-calculator/

142. **Correct Answer:** *BC*

The hardware related jobs is the prime responsibility of AWS. VPC network access control lists is something a customer has to do himself to secure the applications. Encrypting data in transit and at rest is a shared responsibility in which AWS plays a part. All hardware related jobs have nothing to do with the customer.

Reference:
https://dzone.com/articles/aws-shared-responsibility-model-cloud-security

143. **Correct Answer:** *AB*

Reference:
https://wa.aws.amazon.com/wat.concept.elasticity.en.html

144. **Correct Answer:** *A*

The key to understanding spot instances is to look at the way that cloud service providers such as Amazon Web Services (AWS) operate. Cloud service providers invest in hardware resources and then release those resources (often on a per-hour basis) to subscribers. One of the problems with this business model, however, is that at any given time, there are likely to be compute resources that are not being utilized. These resources represent hardware capacity that AWS has paid for but are sitting idle, and not making AWS any money at the moment.

Rather than allowing these computing resources to go to waste, AWS offers them at a substantially discounted rate, with the understanding that if someone needs those resources for running a normal EC2 instance, that instance will take priority over spot instances that are using the hardware resources at a discounted rate.

In fact, spot instances will be stopped if the resources are needed elsewhere.

Reference:
https://awsinsider.net/articles/2017/09/25/aws-spot-instances-primer.aspx

145. **Correct Answer:** *BC*

146. **Correct Answer:** *D*

AWS Lambda is charging its users by the number of requests for their functions and by the duration, which is the time the code needs to execute. When code starts running in response to an event, AWS Lambda counts a request. It will charge the total number of requests across all of the functions used. Duration is calculated by the time when your code started executing until it returns or until it is terminated, rounded up near to 100ms. The AWS Lambda pricing depends on the amount of memory that the user used to allocate to the function.

Reference:
https://dashbird.io/blog/aws-lambda-pricing-model-explained/

147. **Correct Answer: A**

AWS Security Groups act like a firewall for your Amazon EC2 instances controlling both inbound and outbound trafic. When you launch an instance on Amazon

EC2, you need to assign it to a particular security group.

After that, you can set up ports and protocols, which remain open for users and computers over the internet.

AWS Security Groups are very flexible. You can use the default security group and still customize it according to your liking (although we don›t recommend this practice because groups should be named according to their purpose.) Or you can create a security group that you want for your specific applications. To do this, you can write the corresponding code or use the Amazon EC2 console to make the process easier.

Reference:

https://www.threatstack.com/blog/aws-security-groups-what-they-are-and-how-to-get-the-most-out-of-them

148. **Correct Answer: D**

- Backup and Restore: a simple, straightforward, cost-effective method that backs up and restores data as needed. Keep in mind that because none of your data is on standby, this method, while cheap, can be quite time-consuming.

- Pilot Light: This method keeps critical applications and data at the ready so that it can be quickly retrieved if needed.

- Warm Standby: This method keeps a duplicate version of your business core elements running on standby at all times, which makes for a little downtime and an almost seamless transition.

- Multi-Site Solution: Also known as a Hot Standby, this method fully replicates your company›s data/applications between two or more active locations and splits your trafic/usage between them. If a disaster strikes, everything is simply rerouted to the unaffected area, which means you›ll suffer almost zero downtime. However, by running two separate environments simultaneously, you will obviously incur much higher costs.

Reference:

https://cloudranger.com/best-practices-aws-disaster-recovery-planning/

149. **Correct Answer:** *B*

AWS TCO calculators allow you to estimate the cost savings when using AWS and provide a detailed set of reports that can be used in executive presentations. The calculators also give you the option to modify assumptions that best meet your business needs.

Reference: https://aws.amazon.com/tco-calculator/

150. **Correct Answer:** *B*

The way that Reserved Instance discounts apply to accounts in an organization's consolidated billing family depends on whether Reserved Instance sharing is turned on or off for the account. By default, Reserved Instance sharing for all accounts in an organization is turned on. You can change this setting by Turning Off

Reserved Instance Sharing for an account.

The capacity reservation for a Reserved Instance applies only to the account the Reserved Instance was purchased on, regardless of whether Reserved Instance sharing is turned on or off.

Reference:

https://aws.amazon.com/premiumsupport/knowledge-center/ec2-ri-consolidated-billing/

151. **Correct Answer:** *B*

You can use the consolidated billing feature in AWS Organizations to consolidate billing and payment for multiple AWS accounts or multiple Amazon Internet

Services Pvt. Ltd (AISPL) accounts. Every organization in AWS Organizations has a master (payer) account that pays the charges of all the member (linked) accounts.

Reference:

https://docs.aws.amazon.com/awsaccountbilling/latest/aboutv2/consolidated-billing.html

152. **Correct Answer:** *A*

Use AWS Local Zones to deploy workloads closer to your end-users for low-latency requirements. AWS Local Zones have their own connection to the internet and support AWS Direct Connect, so resources created in the Local Zone can serve local end-users with very low-latency communications. nation

Reference:

https://aws.amazon.com/about-aws/global-infrastructure/localzones/faqs/

153. **Correct Answer:** *C*

The cloud allows you to trade capital expenses (such as data centers and physical servers) for variable expenses, and only pay for IT as you consume it. Plus, the variable expenses are much lower than what you would pay to do it yourself because of the economies of scale.

Reference:

https://aws.amazon.com/what-is-cloud-computing/

154. **Correct Answer:** *B*

AWS assets are centrally managed through an inventory management system that stores and tracks owner, location, status, maintenance, and descriptive information for AWS-owned assets. Following procurement, assets are scanned and tracked, and assets undergoing maintenance are checked and monitored for ownership, status, and resolution.

Reference:

https://aws.amazon.com/compliance/data-center/controls/

155. **Correct Answer:** *C*

Reference:

https://aws.amazon.com/blogs/aws/cross-region-read-replicas-for-amazon-rds-for-mysql/

156. **Correct Answer:** *C*

When you create IAM policies, follow the standard security advice of granting least privilege, or granting only the permissions required to perform a task.

Determine what users (and roles) need to do and then craft policies that allow them to perform only those tasks.

Reference:

https://docs.aws.amazon.com/IAM/latest/UserGuide/best-practices.html

157. **Correct Answer:** *BD*

158. **Correct Answer:** *C*

Reference:

https://aws.amazon.com/compliance/shared-responsibility-model/

159. **Correct Answer:** *B*

AWS offers premium services such as AWS Trusted Advisor, which provides real-time guidance to help you reduce cost, increase performance, and improve security.

Reference:

https://www.ibm.com/downloads/cas/2N40X4PQ

160. **Correct Answer:** *D*

Support for monitoring the health of each service independently, as health checks are defined at the target group level and many CloudWatch metrics are reported at the target group level. Attaching a target group to an Auto Scaling group enables you to scale each service dynamically based on demand.

Reference:

https://docs.aws.amazon.com/elasticloadbalancing/latest/application/introduction.html

161. **Correct Answer:** *CE*

With the basic Cloud infrastructure secured and maintained by AWS, the responsibility for what goes into the cloud falls on you. This covers both client and server side encryption and network trafic protection, security of the operating system, network, and firewall configuration, followed by application security and identity and access management.

Firewall configuration remains the responsibility of the end user, which integrates at the platform and application management level. For example, RDS utilizes security groups, which you would be responsible for configuring and implementing.

Reference:
https://cloudacademy.com/blog/aws-shared-responsibility-model-security/

162. **Correct Answer:** C

The AWS Storage Gateway service enables hybrid cloud storage between on-premises environments and the AWS Cloud. It seamlessly integrates on-premises enterprise applications and workflows with Amazon›s block and object cloud storage services through industry standard storage protocols. It provides low-latency performance by caching frequently accessed data on premises, while storing data securely and durably in Amazon cloud storage services. It provides an optimized data transfer mechanism and bandwidth management, which tolerates unreliable networks and minimizes the amount of data being transferred. It brings the security, manageability, durability, and scalability of AWS to existing enterprise environments through native integration with AWS encryption, identity management, monitoring, and storage services.

Typical use cases include backup and archiving, disaster recovery, moving data to S3 for in-cloud workloads, and tiered storage.

Reference:
https://aws.amazon.com/storagegateway/faqs/

163. **Correct Answer:** *C*

Reference:
https://cloudacademy.com/blog/aws-shared-responsibility-model-security/

164. **Correct Answer:** *B*

Amazon RDS Multi-AZ deployments provide enhanced availability and durability for Database (DB) Instances, making them a natural fit for production database workloads. When you provision a Multi-AZ DB Instance, Amazon RDS automatically creates a primary DB Instance and synchronously replicates the data to a standby instance in a different Availability Zone (AZ). Each AZ runs on its own physically distinct, independent infrastructure, and is engineered to be highly reliable. In case of an infrastructure failure, Amazon RDS performs an automatic failover to the standby (or to a read replica in the case of Amazon Aurora), so that you can resume database operations as soon as the failover   is complete. Since the endpoint for your DB Instance remains the same after a failover, your application can resume database operation without the need for manual administrative intervention.

Reference: https://aws.amazon.com/rds/details/multi-az/

165. **Correct Answer:** *D*

When you create IAM policies, follow the standard security advice of granting least privilege, or granting only the permissions required to perform a task.

Determine what users (and roles) need to do and then craft policies that allow them to perform only those tasks.

Reference:

https://docs.aws.amazon.com/IAM/latest/UserGuide/best-practices.html#grant-least-privilege

166. **Correct Answer:** *C*

IT systems should ideally be designed in a way that reduces inter-dependencies. Your components need to be loosely coupled to avoid changes or failure in one of the components from affecting others.

Your infrastructure also needs to have well defined interfaces that allow the various components to interact with each other only through specific, technology- agnostic interfaces. Modifying any underlying operations without affecting other components should be made possible.

Reference:

https://www.botmetric.com/blog/aws-cloud-architecture-design-principles/

167. **Correct Answer:** *B*

Amazon VPC provides multiple network connectivity options for you to leverage depending on your current network designs and requirements. These connectivity options include leveraging either the internet or an AWS Direct Connect connection as the network backbone and   terminating the connection into either AWS or user-managed network endpoints. Additionally, with AWS, you can choose how network routing is delivered between Amazon VPC and your networks, leveraging either AWS or user-managed network equipment and routes.

Reference:

https://docs.aws.amazon.com/whitepapers/latest/aws-vpc-connectivity-options/introduction.html

168. **Correct Answer:** *C*

169. **Correct Answer:** *BC*

Your root account should always be protected by Multi-Factor Authentication (MFA). This additional layer of security helps protect against unauthorized logins to your account by requiring two factors: something you know (a password) and something you have (for example, an MFA device). AWS supports virtual and hardware MFA devices and U2F security keys.

Cognito can be used as an Identity Provider (IdP), where it stores and maintains users and credentials securely for your applications, or it can be integrated with

OpenID Connect, SAML, and other popular web identity providers like Amazon.com.

Using Amazon Cognito, you can generate temporary access credentials for your clients to access AWS services, eliminating the need to store long-term credentials in client applications.

Reference:

https://aws.amazon.com/blogs/security/guidelines-for-protecting-your-aws-account-while-using-programmatic-access/

170. **Correct Answer:** *D*

To improve control over your AWS environment, you can use AWS Organizations to create groups of accounts, and then attach policies to a group to ensure the correct policies are applied across the accounts without requiring custom scripts and manual processes.

Reference:

https://aws.amazon.com/organizations/

171. **Correct Answer:** *B*

Reference:
https://docs.aws.amazon.com/AmazonCloudWatch/latest/monitoring/monitor_estimated_charges_with_cloudwatch.html

172. **Correct Answer:** *A*

You can use AWS Artifact Reports to download AWS security and compliance documents, such as AWS ISO certifications, Payment Card Industry (PCI), and System and Organization Control (SOC) reports.

Reference: https://aws.amazon.com/artifact/faq/

173. **Correct Answer:** *A*

Reference: https://aws.amazon.com/premiumsupport/plans/

174. **Correct Answer:** *B*

Reference: https://aws.amazon.com/blogs/apn/the-5-pillars-of-the-aws-well-architected-framework/

175. **Correct Answer:** *B*

When you stop or terminate an instance, every block of storage in the instance store is reset. Therefore, your data cannot be accessed through the instance store of another instance.

Reference:
https://docs.aws.amazon.com/AWSEC2/latest/UserGuide/InstanceStorage.html

176. **Correct Answer:** *A*

Reference:https://data-flair.training/blogs/aws-advantages/

177. **Correct Answer:** *B*

178. **Correct Answer:** *D*

There are six design principles for operational excellence in the cloud:
- Perform operations as code
- Annotate documentation
- Make frequent, small, reversible changes Refine operations procedures frequently
- Anticipate failure
- Learn from all operational failures Reference:

https://aws.amazon.com/blogs/apn/the-5-pillars-of-the-aws-well-architected-framework/

179. **Correct Answer:** *A*

Reference: https://aws.amazon.com/tools/

180. **Correct Answer:** *A*

With On-Demand instances, you pay for compute capacity by the hour or the second depending on which instances you run. No longer-term commitments or upfront payments are needed. You can increase or decrease your compute capacity depending on the demands of your application and only pay the specified per hourly rates for the instance you use.

Reference:
https://aws.amazon.com/ec2/pricing/

181. **Correct Answer:** *D*

Amazon Aurora is a relational database service that combines the speed and availability of high-end commercial databases with the simplicity and cost- effectiveness of open source databases. The MySQL-compatible edition of Aurora delivers up to 5X the throughput of standard MySQL running on the same hardware, and enables existing MySQL applications and tools to run without requiring modification.

Amazon Aurora will automatically grow the size of your database volume as your database storage needs grow. Your volume will grow in increments of 10 GB up to a maximum of 64 TB. You don't need to provision excess storage for your database to handle future growth.

Reference:

https://aws.amazon.com/rds/aurora/mysql-features/

182. Correct Answer: C

A VPC peering connection is a networking connection between two VPCs that enables you to route trafic between them using private IPv4 addresses or IPv6 addresses. Instances in either VPC can communicate with each other as if they are within the same network. You can create a VPC peering connection between your own VPCs, or with a VPC in another AWS account. The VPCs can be in different regions (also known as an inter-region VPC peering connection).

Reference:

https://docs.aws.amazon.com/vpc/latest/peering/what-is-vpc-peering.html

183. Correct Answer: D

AWS CodeCommit is a version control service hosted by Amazon Web Services that you can use to privately store and manage assets (such as documents, source code, and binary files) in the cloud.

Reference:

https://docs.aws.amazon.com/codecommit/latest/userguide/welcome.html

184. **Correct Answer:** *B*

TCO calculator compare the cost of running your applications in an on-premises or colocation environment to AWS.

Reference:
https://awstcocalculator.com

185. **Correct Answer:** *D*

AWS Snowmobile is an exabyte-scale data transfer service that can move extremely large amounts of data to AWS in a fast, secure, and cost- effective manner.

You can transfer up to 100PB per Snowmobile, a 45-foot long ruggedized shipping container, pulled by a semi-trailer truck. Snowmobile makes it easy to move massive volumes of data to the cloud, including video libraries, image repositories, or even a complete data center migration. All data is encrypted with 256-bit encryption and you can manage your encryption keys with AWS Key Management Service (AWS KMS). Snowmobile includes GPS tracking, alarm monitoring, 24/7 video surveillance and an optional escort security vehicle while in transit.

Reference:
https://aws.amazon.com/about-aws/whats-new/2016/11/
move-exabyte-scale-data-sets-with-aws-snowmobile/

186. **Correct Answer:** *BE*

Reference:
https://d0.awsstatic.com/whitepapers/aws_pricing_overview.
pdf

187. **Correct Answer:** *CE*

Elastic Load Balancing supports the following types of load balancers: Application Load Balancers, Network Load Balancers, and Classic Load Balancers.

Amazon ECS services can use either type of load balancer. Application Load Balancers are used to route HTTP/HTTPS (or Layer 7) trafic. Network Load Balancers and Classic Load Balancers are used to route TCP (or Layer 4) trafic.

Reference:
https://docs.aws.amazon.com/AmazonECS/latest/developerguide/load-balancer-types.html

188. **Correct Answer:** *B*

AWS offers you a pay-as-you-go approach for pricing for over 160 cloud services. With AWS you pay only for the individual services you need,   for as long as you use them, and without requiring long-term contracts or complex licensing. AWS pricing is similar to how you pay for utilities   like water and electricity. You only pay for the services you consume, and once you stop using them, there are no additional costs or termination fees.

Reference:
https://aws.amazon.com/pricing/

189. **Correct Answer:** *B*

You can deliver content and decrease end-user latency of your web application using Amazon CloudFront. Cloud-Front speeds up content   delivery by leveraging its global network of data centers, known as edge locations, to reduce delivery time by caching your content close to your end users. CloudFront fetches your content from an origin, such as an Amazon S3 bucket, an Amazon EC2 instance, an Amazon

Elastic Load Balancing load balancer or your own web server, when it's not already in an edge location. CloudFront can be used to deliver your entire website or application, including dynamic, static, streaming, and interactive content.

Reference:
https://aws.amazon.com/getting-started/tutorials/deliver-content-faster/

190. **Correct Answer:** *D*

AWS Artifact is your go-to, central resource for compliance-related information that matters to you. It provides on-demand access to AWS security and compliance reports and select online agreements. Reports available in AWS Artifact include our Service Organization Control (SOC) reports, Payment Card

Industry (PCI) reports, and certifications from accreditation bodies across geographies and compliance verticals that validate the implementation and operating effectiveness of AWS security controls. Agreements available in AWS Artifact include the Business Associate Addendum (BAA) and the Nondisclosure Agreement (NDA).

Reference: https://aws.amazon.com/artifact/

191. **Correct Answer:** *D*

Reference:
https://severalnines.com/news/aws-users-prefer-self-managed-databases

192. **Correct Answer:** *B*

Reference: https://aws.amazon.com/premiumsupport/plans/enterprise/

193. **Correct Answer:** *C*

An AWS Region is a geographic location where AWS provides multiple, physically separated and isolated Availability Zones which are connected with low latency, high throughput, and highly redundant networking.

Reference:
https://aws.amazon.com/s3/faqs/

194. **Correct Answer:** *A*

You can continue to optimize your spend and keep your development costs low by making sure you revisit your architecture often, to adjust to your startup growth.

Manage your cost further by leveraging different options such as S3 CloudFront for caching & oPoading to reduce cost of EC2 computing, as well as Elastic Load

Balancing which prepares you for massive scale, high reliability and uninterrupted growth. Another way to keep costs down is to use AWS Identity and Access

Management solutions (IAM) to manage governance of your cost drivers effectively and by the right teams.

Reference:
https://aws.amazon.com/startups/lean/

195. **Correct Answer:** *D*

Agile is a time boxed, iterative approach to software delivery that builds software incrementally from the start of the project, instead of trying to deliver it all at once near the end.

Reference: http://www.agilenutshell.com

196. **Correct Answer:** *D*

197. **Correct Answer:** *AD*

Reference: https://aws.amazon.com/shield/

198. **Correct Answer:** *ACE*

Reference:
https://aws.amazon.com/blogs/aws/the-new-aws-tco-calculator/

199. **Correct Answer:** *B*

Rekognition Image is an image recognition service that detects objects, scenes, and faces; extracts text; recognizes celebrities; and identifies inappropriate content in images. It also allows you to search and compare faces. Rekognition Image is based on the same proven, highly scalable, deep learning technology developed by Amazon›s computer vision scientists to analyze billions of images daily for Prime Photos.

Reference:
https://aws.amazon.com/rekognition/faqs/

200. **Correct Answer:** *A*

Reference: https://www.awstcocalculator.com/Output/Load/f85bbf7e131446643911859504

201. **Correct Answer:** *D*

Reference:
https://cloudacademy.com/blog/aws-shared-responsibility-model-security/

202. **Correct Answer:** *B*

To forecast your costs, use the AWS Cost Explorer. Use cost allocation tags to divide your resources into groups, and then estimate the costs for each group.

Reference:

https://aws.amazon.com/premiumsupport/knowledge-center/estimating-aws-resource-costs/

203. **Correct Answer:** *B*

204. **Correct Answer:** *B*

You can monitor your estimated AWS charges by using Amazon CloudWatch. When you enable the monitoring of estimated charges for your AWS account, the estimated charges are calculated and sent several times daily to CloudWatch as metric data. Billing metric data is stored in the US East (N. Virginia) Region and represents worldwide charges. This data includes the estimated charges for every service in AWS that you use, in addition to the estimated overall total of your AWS charges.

Reference:

https://docs.aws.amazon.com/AmazonCloudWatch/latest/monitoring/monitor_estimated_charges_with_cloudwatch.html

205. **Correct Answer:** *C*

Reference:

https://aws.amazon.com/ec2/pricing/reserved-instances/

206. **Correct Answer:** *B*

Media storage devices used to store customer data are classified by AWS as Critical and treated accordingly, as high impact, throughout their life-cycles. AWS has exacting standards on how to install, service, and eventually destroy the devices when they are no longer useful. When a storage device has reached the end of its useful life, AWS decommissions media using techniques detailed in NIST 800-88. Media that stored customer data is not removed from AWS control until it has been securely decommissioned.

Reference:

https://aws.amazon.com/compliance/data-center/controls/

207. **Correct Answer:** *C*

AWS manages dozens of compliance programs in its infrastructure. This means that segments of your compliance have already been completed.

Reference:

https://docs.aws.amazon.com/whitepapers/latest/aws-overview/security-and-compliance.html

208. **Correct Answer:** *D*

Amazon CloudFront is a fast content delivery network (CDN) service that securely delivers data, videos, applications, and APIs to customers globally with low latency, high transfer speeds, all within a developer-friendly environment. CloudFront is integrated with AWS both physical locations that are directly connected to the AWS global infrastructure, as well as other AWS services.

Reference:

https://aws.amazon.com/cloudfront/

209. **Correct Answer:** *AD*

Reference:

https://docs.aws.amazon.com/AWSCloudFormation/latest/UserGuide/deploying.applications.html

210. **Correct Answer:** *C*

The TCO Calculator provides directional guidance on possible realized savings when deploying AWS. This tool is built on an underlying calculation model, that generates a fair assessment of value that a customer may achieve given the data provided by the user.

Reference:

https://aws.amazon.com/tco-calculator/

211. **Correct Answer:** *AB*

Reference:

https://aws.amazon.com/blogs/apn/the-5-pillars-of-the-aws-well-architected-framework/

212. **Correct Answer:** *AE*

Reference:

https://aws.amazon.com/premiumsupport/knowledge-center/potential-account-compromise/

213. **Correct Answer:** *B*

Reference:

https://aws.amazon.com/blogs/startups/high-availability-for-mere-mortals/

214. **Correct Answer:** *D*

AWS Shield is a managed Distributed Denial of Service (DDoS) protection service that safeguards applications running on AWS. AWS Shield provides always-on detection and automatic inline mitigations that minimize application downtime and latency, so there is no need to engage AWS Support to benefit from DDoS protection. There are two tiers of AWS Shield - Standard and Advanced.

Reference:

https://aws.amazon.com/shield/

215. **Correct Answer:** *B*

With Basic monitoring you get data on your cloudwatch metrics every 5 minutes. Enabling detailed monitoring, you will get the data every one minute.

To check if detailed monitoring is enabled, on your EC2 Console, Select the instance, on the lower plane, Select Monitoring.

Reference:

https://forums.aws.amazon.com/thread.jspa?threadID=263876

216. **Correct Answer:** *C*

AWS Identity and Access Management (IAM) enables you to manage access to AWS services and resources securely. Using IAM, you can create and manage

AWS users and groups, and use permissions to allow and deny their access to AWS resources.

Reference:

https://aws.amazon.com/iam/

217. **Correct Answer:** *AE*

Reference:

https://aws.amazon.com/premiumsupport/knowledge-center/ec2-ri-basics/

218. **Correct Answer:** *B*

When the unhealthy Availability Zone returns to a healthy state, Auto Scaling automatically redistributes the application instances evenly across all of the designated Availability Zones.

Reference:

https://docs.aws.amazon.com/autoscaling/ec2/userguide/auto-scaling-benefits.html

219. **Correct Answer:** *B*

The account that originally purchased the Reserved Instance receives the discount first. If the purchasing account doesn't have any instances that match the terms of the Reserved Instance, the discount for the Reserved Instance is assigned to any matching usage on another account in the organization.

Reference:

https://aws.amazon.com/premiumsupport/knowledge-center/ec2-ri-consolidated-billing/

220. **Correct Answer:** *B*

Reference:

https://aws.amazon.com/about-aws/whats-new/2017/10/announcing-amazon-ec2-per-second-billing/

221. **Correct Answer:** *AB*

Reference:

https://docs.aws.amazon.com/whitepapers/latest/aws-overview/compute-services.html

222. **Correct Answer:** *B*

AWS CloudFormation provides a common language for you to model and provision AWS and third party application resources in your cloud environment. AWS

CloudFormation allows you to use programming languages or a simple text file to model and provision, in an automated and secure manner, all the resources needed for your applications across all regions and accounts. This gives you a single source of truth for your AWS and third party resources.

Reference:
https://aws.amazon.com/cloudformation/

223. **Correct Answer:** *BD*

Reference: https://aws.amazon.com/hybrid/

224. **Correct Answer:** *B*

AWS Direct Connect lets you establish a dedicated network connection between your network and one of the AWS Direct Connect locations. Using industry standard 802.1q VLANs, this dedicated connection can be partitioned into multiple virtual interfaces. This allows you to use the same connection to access public resources such as objects stored in Amazon S3 using public IP address space, and private resources such as Amazon EC2 instances running within an Amazon

Virtual Private Cloud (VPC) using private IP space, while maintaining network separation between the public and private environments. Virtual interfaces can be reconfigured at any time to meet your changing needs.

Reference:
https://aws.amazon.com/directconnect/

225. **Correct Answer:** *AB*

Reference:
https://www.edureka.co/community/600/what-is-an-edge-location-in-aws

226. **Correct Answer:** *B*

Amazon Virtual Private Cloud (Amazon VPC) is a logically isolated, private section of the AWS Cloud to launch resources in a virtual data center in the cloud.

Amazon VPC allows you to leverage multiple Availability Zones (AZ) within a region so that you can build greater fault tolerance within your workloads. You have complete control.

Reference:

https://aws.amazon.com/blogs/publicsector/aws-networking-capabilities-gives-you-choices-for-hybrid-cloud-connectivity-but-which-service- works-best- for-your-use-case/

227. **Correct Answer:** *D*

Reference:

https://aws.amazon.com/tco-calculator/

228. **Correct Answer:** *AB*

Reference:

https://aws.amazon.com/partners/aws-marketplace/

229. **Correct Answer:** *B*

Loosely coupled architectures reduce interdependencies, so that a change or failure in a component does not cascade to other components.

Reference:

https://aws-certified-cloud-practitioner.fandom.com/wiki/1.3_List_the_different_cloud_architecture_design_principles

230. **Correct Answer:** *BE*

Reference:

https://aws.amazon.com/compliance/shared-responsibility-model/

231. **Correct Answer:** *D*

AWS Config is a service that enables you to assess, audit, and evaluate the configurations of your AWS resources. Config continuously monitors and records your

AWS resource configurations and allows you to automate the evaluation of recorded configurations against desired configurations. With Config, you can review changes in configurations and relationships between AWS resources, dive into detailed resource configuration histories, and determine your overall compliance against the configurations specified in your internal guidelines. This enables you to simplify compliance auditing, security analysis, change management, and operational troubleshooting.

Reference:

https://aws.amazon.com/config/

232. **Correct Answer:** *B*

233. **Correct Answer:** *C*

AWS maintains the configuration of its infrastructure devices, but a customer is responsible for configuring their own guest operating systems, databases, and applications.

Reference:

https://aws.amazon.com/compliance/shared-responsibility-model/

234. **Correct Answer:** *C*

Amazon CloudFront is a fast content delivery network (CDN) service that securely delivers data, videos, applications, and APIs to customers globally with low latency, high transfer speeds, all within a developer-friendly environment. CloudFront is integrated with AWS both physical locations that are directly connected to the AWS global infrastructure, as well as other AWS services.

Reference: https://aws.amazon.com/cloudfront/

235. **Correct Answer:** *C*

Reference: https://wa.aws.amazon.com/wat.map.en.html

236. **Correct Answer:** *D*

Reference:
https://aws.amazon.com/premiumsupport/knowledge-center/report-aws-abuse/

237. **Correct Answer:** *AC*

238. **Correct Answer:** *B*

Reference:
https://docs.aws.amazon.com/IAM/latest/UserGuide/id_credentials_access-keys.html

239. **Correct Answer:** *C*

AWS Trusted Advisor is an online tool that provides you real time guidance to help you provision your resources following AWS best practices. Whether establishing new workflows, developing applications, or as part of ongoing improvement, take advantage of the recommendations provided by Trusted

Advisor on a regular basis to help keep your solutions provisioned optimally.

Reference:
https://aws.amazon.com/premiumsupport/technology/trusted-advisor/

240. **Correct Answer:** *B*

AWS Cost Explorer has an easy-to-use interface that lets you visualize, understand, and manage your AWS costs and usage over time.

Reference:
https://aws.amazon.com/aws-cost-management/aws-cost-explorer/

241. **Correct Answer:** *B*

AWS Artifact is your go-to, central resource for compliance-related information that matters to you. It provides on-demand access to AWS security and compliance reports and select online agreements. Reports available in AWS Artifact include our Service Organization Control (SOC) reports, Payment Card Industry (PCI) reports, and certifications from accreditation bodies across geographies and compliance verticals that validate the implementation and operating effectiveness of AWS security controls. Agreements available in AWS Artifact include the Business Associate Addendum (BAA) and the Nondisclosure Agreement(NDA).

Reference: https://aws.amazon.com/artifact/

242. **Correct Answer:** *AC*

Reference:
https://aws.amazon.com/comprehend/features/ https://aws.amazon.com/cloudfront/

243. **Correct Answer:** *B*

Upload your code and Elastic Beanstalk automatically handles the deployment, from capacity provisioning, load balancing, auto-scaling to application health monitoring. At the same time, you retain full control over the AWS resources powering your application and can access the underlying resources at any time.

Reference:

https://aws.amazon.com/elasticbeanstalk/

244. **Correct Answer:** *C*

Reference:

https://docs.aws.amazon.com/vpc/latest/userguide/VPC_Security.html

245. **Correct Answer:** *B*

Reference:

https://docs.aws.amazon.com/AWSEC2/latest/UserGuide/using-regions-availability-zones.html

246. **Correct Answer:** *A*

Reference:

https://www.10thmagnitude.com/opex-vs-capex-the-real-cloud-computing-cost-advantage/

247. **Correct Answer:** *B*

Reference:

https://cloudacademy.com/blog/aws-shared-responsibility-model-security/

248. **Correct Answer:** *B*

You can use the consolidated billing feature in AWS Organizations to consolidate billing and payment for multiple AWS accounts or multiple Amazon Internet Services Pvt. Ltd (AISPL) accounts. Every organization in AWS Organizations has a master (payer) account that pays the charges of all the member (linked) accounts.

Reference:
https://docs.aws.amazon.com/awsaccountbilling/latest/aboutv2/consolidated-billing.html

249. **Correct Answer:** *B*

Reference:
https://aws.amazon.com/compliance/shared-responsibility-model/

250. **Correct Answer:** *D*

Reference: https://aws.amazon.com/premiumsupport/faqs/

251. **Correct Answer:** *BC*

Reference:
https://d1.awsstatic.com/whitepapers/architecture/AWS_Well-Architected_Framework.pdf (5)

252. **Correct Answer:** *D*

Reference:
https://aws.amazon.com/ec2/pricing/reserved-instances/pricing/

253. **Correct Answer:** *B*

Reference:

https://docs.aws.amazon.com/AWSEC2/latest/UserGuide/using-regions-availability-zones.html

254. **Correct Answer:** *B*

Reference:

https://aws.amazon.com/premiumsupport/knowledge-center/estimating-aws-resource-costs/

255. **Correct Answer:** *BD*

Reference:

https://aws.amazon.com/blogs/apn/amazon-vpc-for-on-premises-network-engineers-part-one/

256. **Correct Answer:** *D*

AWS WAF is a web application firewall that helps protect web applications from common web exploits that could affect application availability, compromise security, or consume excessive resources. You can use AWS WAF to define customizable web security rules that control which trafic accesses your web applications. If you use AWS Shield Advanced, you can use AWS WAF at no extra cost for those protected resources and can engage the DRT to create WAF rules.

Reference:

https://aws.amazon.com/answers/networking/aws-ddos-attack-mitigation/

257. **Correct Answer:** *D*

Reference:

https://asperbrothers.com/blog/infrastructure-as-code-aws/

258. **Correct Answer:** *B*

You can use AWS Direct Connect to establish a private virtual interface from your on-premise network directly to your Amazon VPC, providing you with a private, high bandwidth network connection between your network and your VPC. With multiple virtual interfaces, you can even establish private connectivity to multiple VPCs while maintaining network isolation.

Reference:https://aws.amazon.com/directconnect/

259. **Correct Answer:** *D*

Amazon Athena is defined is an interactive query service that makes it easy to analyse data directly in Amazon Simple Storage Service (Amazon S3) using standard SQL. So, it›s another SQL query engine for large data sets stored in S3. This is very similar to other SQL query engines, such as Apache Drill. But unlike Apache Drill, Athena is limited to data only from Amazon's own S3 storage service. However, Athena is able to query a variety of file formats, including, but not limited to CSV, Parquet, JSON, etc.

260. **Correct Answer:** *A*

AWS CloudFormation provides a common language for you to model and provision AWS and third party application resources in your cloud environment. AWS

CloudFormation allows you to use programming languages or a simple text file to model and provision, in an automated and secure manner, all the resources needed for your applications across all regions and accounts. This gives you a single source of truth for your AWS and third party resources.

Reference:
https://aws.amazon.com/cloudformation/

261. **Correct Answer:** *A*

Reference:
https://www.sisense.com/glossary/redshift-database/

262. **Correct Answer:** *B*

Reference:
https://docs.aws.amazon.com/AWSEC2/latest/
WindowsGuide/ec2-security-groups.html

263. **Correct Answer:** *CD*

264. **Correct Answer:** *D*

Amazon Inspector is an automated security assessment service that helps improve the security and compliance of applications deployed on AWS. Amazon

Inspector automatically assesses applications for exposure, vulnerabilities, and deviations from best practices. After performing an assessment, Amazon Inspector produces a detailed list of security findings prioritized by level of severity. These findings can be reviewed directly or as part of detailed assessment reports which are available via the Amazon Inspector console or API.

Reference:
https://aws.amazon.com/inspector/

265. **Correct Answer:** *B*

Reference:
https://aws.amazon.com/answers/account-management/aws-multi-account-billing-strategy/

266. **Correct Answer:** *A*

AWS Service Catalog Delivery Partners are APN Consulting Partners who help create catalogs of IT services that are approved by the customer's organization for use on AWS. With AWS Service Catalog, customers and partners can centrally manage commonly deployed IT services to help achieve consistent governance and meet compliance requirements while enabling users to self-provision approved services.

Reference: https://aws.amazon.com/servicecatalog/partners/

267. **Correct Answer:** *D*

S3 Glacier Deep Archive is Amazon S3's lowest-cost storage class and supports long-term retention and digital preservation for data that may be accessed once or twice in a year. It is designed for customers particularly those in highly-regulated industries, such as the Financial Services, Healthcare, and Public Sectors that retain data sets for 7-10 years or longer to meet regulatory compliance requirements. S3 Glacier Deep Archive can also be used for backup and disaster recovery use cases, and is a cost-effective and easy-to-manage alternative to magnetic tape systems, whether they are on-premises libraries or off-premises services.

Reference: https://aws.amazon.com/s3/storage-classes/

268. **Correct Answer:** *BD*

269. **Correct Answer:** *B*

Amazon Macie is a security service that uses machine learning to automatically discover, classify, and protect sensitive data in AWS. Macie recognizes sensitive data such as personally identifiable information (PII) or intellectual property. It provides you with dashboards and alerts that give visibility into how this data is being accessed or moved.

Reference:

https://docs.aws.amazon.com/macie/latest/userguide/what-is-macie.html

270. **Correct Answer:** *D*

Moving data to the cloud is not quite as simple as flipping a switch. For companies that have managed their own data centers or server rooms for decades, there are a few steps to consider -- and it's not always wise to pull the plug on an internal infrastructure quite so quickly. If a startup uses on-premise business servers and then experiences unexpected growth, abandoning those servers doesn›t make sense (even if the long-term plan is to do exactly that).

AWS Storage Gateway is a way to bridge this gap for companies of any size. It›s a hybrid storage option that connects on-premise storage including age-old tape backup systems to the cloud in a way that also provides one console to access all storage configurations.

Reference:

https://www.techradar.com/news/what-is-aws-storage-gateway

271. **Correct Answer:** *C*

Reference:

https://docs.aws.amazon.com/AWSEC2/latest/UserGuide/using-regions-availability-zones.html

272. **Correct Answer:** *B*

Reference:

https://wa.aws.amazon.com/wat.question.REL_7.en.html

273. **Correct Answer:** *A*

You can use AWS Direct Connect to establish a private virtual interface from your on-premise network directly to your Amazon VPC, providing you with a private, high bandwidth network connection between your network and your VPC. With multiple virtual interfaces, you can even establish private connectivity to multiple VPCs while maintaining network isolation.

Reference:https://aws.amazon.com/directconnect/

274. **Correct Answer:** *C*

Security and Compliance is a shared responsibility between AWS and the customer. This shared model can help relieve the customer›s operational burden as

AWS operates, manages and controls the components from the host operating system and virtualization layer down to the physical security of the facilities in which the service operates.

Reference:
https://aws.amazon.com/compliance/shared-responsibility-model/

275. **Correct Answer:** *B*

276. **Correct Answer:** *C*

Reference:
https://docs.aws.amazon.com/kms/latest/developerguide/services-ebs.html

277. **Correct Answer:** *AC*

278. **Correct Answer:** *BE*

279. **Correct Answer:** *B*

AWS Shield Standard provides protection for all AWS customers from common, most frequently occurring network and transport layer DDoS attacks that target your web site or application at no additional charge.

Reference:https://aws.amazon.com/shield/pricing/

280. **Correct Answer:** *C*

Reference:
https://aws.amazon.com/pricing/cost-optimization/

281. **Correct Answer:** *BC*

Reference: https://aws.amazon.com/marketplace

282. **Correct Answer:** *D*

Reference: https://aws.amazon.com/hybrid/

283. **Correct Answer:** *B*

Reference:
https://docs.aws.amazon.com/config/latest/developerguide/
view-manage-resource.html

284. **Correct Answer:** *A*

AWS helps you reduce Total Cost of Ownership (TCO) by reducing the need to invest in large capital expenditures and providing a pay-as-you-go model that empowers you to invest in the capacity you need and use it only when the business requires it.

Reference:
https://aws.amazon.com/tco-calculator/

285. **Correct Answer:** *D*

Reference:
https://aws.amazon.com/blogs/security/the-aws-shared-responsibility-model-and-gdpr/

286. **Correct Answer:** *BC*

Reference:
https://data-flair.training/blogs/aws-advantages/

287. **Correct Answer:** *BC*

Reference:
https://aws.amazon.com/tco-calculator/

288. **Correct Answer:** *B*

Reference:
https://aws.amazon.com/tco-calculator/

289. **Correct Answer:** *C*

Reference:
https://cloudacademy.com/blog/aws-shared-responsibility-model-security/

290. **Correct Answer:** *D*

Reference:
https://docs.aws.amazon.com/whitepapers/latest/aws-overview/six-advantages-of-cloud-computing.html

291. **Correct Answer:** *A*

Reference:
https://d1.awsstatic.com/whitepapers/Migration/aws-migration-whitepaper.pdf

292. **Correct Answer:** *C*

Reference:
https://aws.amazon.com/blogs/mt/automate-account-creation-and-resource-provisioning-using-aws-service-catalog-aws-organizations-and- aws- lambda/

293. **Correct Answer:** *A*

Amazon RDS provides high availability and failover support for DB instances using Multi-AZ deployments. Amazon RDS uses several different technologies to provide failover support. Multi-AZ deployments for Oracle, PostgreSQL, MySQL, and MariaDB DB instances use Amazon's failover technology. SQL Server DB instances use SQL Server Database Mirroring (DBM).

Reference:
https://docs.aws.amazon.com/AmazonRDS/latest/UserGuide/Concepts.MultiAZ.html

294. **Correct Answer:** *A*

Reference: https://aws.amazon.com/premiumsupport/knowledge-center/report-aws-abuse/

295. **Correct Answer:** *A*

AWS CloudTrail is a service that enables governance, compliance, operational auditing, and risk auditing of your AWS account. With CloudTrail, you can log, continuously monitor, and retain account activity related to actions across your AWS infrastructure. CloudTrail provides event history of your AWS account activity, including actions taken through the AWS Management Console, AWS SDKs, command line tools, and other AWS services. This event history simplifies security analysis, resource change tracking, and troubleshooting. In addition, you can use CloudTrail to detect unusual activity in your AWS accounts. These capabilities help simplify operational analysis and troubleshooting.

Reference: https://aws.amazon.com/cloudtrail/

296. **Correct Answer:** *C*

297. **Correct Answer:** *B*

AWS does not require minimum spend commitments or long-term contracts. You replace large upfront expenses with low variable payments that only apply to what you use. With AWS you are not bound to multi-year agreements or complicated licensing models.

Reference:
https://aws.amazon.com/economics/

298. **Correct Answer:** *AC*

Reference:
https://d1.awsstatic.com/whitepapers/AWS_Cloud_Best_Practices.pdf

299. **Correct Answer:** *D*

Use load balancing for oPoading encryption termination (TLS) to improve performance and to manage and route trafic effectively. Distribute trafic across multiple resources or services to allow your workload to take advantage of the elasticity that AWS provides.

Reference:

https://d1.awsstatic.com/whitepapers/architecture/AWS_Well-Architected_Framework.pdf

300. **Correct Answer:** *AB*

Reference:
https://docs.aws.amazon.com/IAM/latest/UserGuide/best-practices.html

301. **Correct Answer:** *CD*

Reference:
https://aws.amazon.com/solutions/aws-landing-zone/

302. **Correct Answer:** *C*

Reference:
https://aws.amazon.com/premiumsupport/plans/enterprise/

303. **Correct Answer:** *A*

304. **Correct Answer:** *B*

Reference: https://aws.amazon.com/ec2/faqs/

305. **Correct Answer:** *C*

Reference:
https://aws.amazon.com/tco-calculator/

306. **Correct Answer:** *A*

Reference:
https://aws.amazon.com/premiumsupport/knowledge-center/ec2-ri-consolidated-billing/

307. **Correct Answer:** *B*

Reference:
https://aws.amazon.com/premiumsupport/knowledge-center/report-aws-abuse/

308. **Correct Answer:** *BD*

Reference: https://aws.amazon.com/cloudfront/faqs/

309. **Correct Answer:** *A*

Reference:
https://blogs.itemis.com/en/serverless-services-on-aws

310. **Correct Answer:** *BD*

Reference:
https://subscription.packtpub.com/book/virtualization_and_
cloud/9781788293723/3/ch03lvl1sec26/vpc-components

311. **Correct Answer:** *B*

312. **Correct Answer:** *CE*

Reference:
https://aws.amazon.com/blogs/security/guidelines-for-
protecting-your-aws-account-while-using-programmatic-
access/

313. **Correct Answer:** *AC*

Reference:
https://aws.amazon.com/premiumsupport/technology/
trusted-advisor/best-practice-checklist/

314. **Correct Answer:** *C*

Reference:
https://docs.aws.amazon.com/kms/latest/developerguide/
control-access.html

315. **Correct Answer:** *BC*

316. **Correct Answer:** *AC*

Reference:

https://aws.amazon.com/compliance/data-center/controls/

317. **Correct Answer:** *B*

Reference:

https://aws.amazon.com/blogs/apn/the-5-pillars-of-the-aws-well-architected-framework/

318. **Correct Answer:** *AD*

Reference:

https://aws.amazon.com/directconnect/

https://aws.amazon.com/blogs/networking-and-content-delivery/introducing-aws-client-vpn-to-securely-access-aws-and-on-premises- resources/

319. **Correct Answer:** *A*

Reference:

https://docs.aws.amazon.com/awsaccountbilling/latest/aboutv2/billing-what-is.html

320. **Correct Answer:** *B*

Reference:

https://docs.aws.amazon.com/whitepapers/latest/aws-overview/global-infrastructure.html

321. **Correct Answer:** *D*

VPC Flow Logs is a feature that enables you to capture information about the IP trafic going to and from network interfaces in your VPC. Flow log data can be published to Amazon CloudWatch Logs or Amazon S3. After you've created a flow log, you can retrieve and view its data in the chosen destination.

Reference:
https://docs.aws.amazon.com/vpc/latest/userguide/flow-logs.html

322. **Correct Answer:** *D*

Reference:
https://aws.amazon.com/blogs/aws/category/auto-scaling/

323. **Correct Answer:** *C*

Reference: https://aws.amazon.com/premiumsupport/plans/

324. **Correct Answer:** *A*

Amazon RDS makes it easy to set up, operate, and scale a relational database in the cloud. It provides cost-eficient and resizable capacity   while automating time- consuming administration tasks, such as hardware provisioning, database setup, patching, and backups. It frees you to focus on your applications, so you can give them the fast performance, high availability, security, and compatibility that they need.

Reference:
https://aws.amazon.com/blogs/database/part-1-role-of-the-dba-when-moving-to-amazon-rds-responsibilities/

325. **Correct Answer:** *C*

Reference:
https://docs.aws.amazon.com/emr/latest/ManagementGuide/emr-plan-region.html

326. **Correct Answer:** *A*

Reference: https://aws.amazon.com/ec2/dedicated-hosts/

327. **Correct Answer:** *CE*

Reference:
https://docs.aws.amazon.com/crypto/latest/userguide/
awscryp-service-hsm.html https://docs.aws.amazon.com/
kms/latest/developerguide/overview.html

328. **Correct Answer:** *A*

Reference:
https://docs.aws.amazon.com/migrationhub/latest/ug/hub-
api.pdf (26)

329. **Correct Answer:** *BD*

330. **Correct Answer:** **B**

The AWS CloudHSM service helps you meet corporate, contractual, and regulatory compliance requirements for data
security by using dedicated Hardware. Security Module
(HSM) instances within the AWS cloud. AWS and AWS Marketplace partners offer a variety of solutions for protecting
sensitive data within the AWS platform, but for some applications and data subject to contractual or regulatory mandates
for managing cryptographic keys, additional protection may
be necessary. CloudHSM complements existing data protection solutions and allows you to protect your encryption keys
within HSMs that are designed and validated to government
standards for secure key management. CloudHSM allows
you to securely generate, store, and manage cryptographic
keys used for data encryption in a way that keys are accessi-
ble only by you.

331. **Correct Answer:** *BE*

Reference:
https://www.whizlabs.com/blog/aws-security-shared-responsibility/

332. **Correct Answer:** *C*

An easy-to-use service for deploying and scaling web applications and web services developed in a number of programming languages. You can configure event notifications for your Elastic Beanstalk environment so that notable events can be automatically published to an SNS topic, then pushed to topic subscribers. As an example, you may use this event-driven architecture to coordinate your continuous integration pipeline (such as Jenkins CI). That way, whenever an environment is created, Elastic Beanstalk publishes this event to an SNS topic, which triggers a subscribing Lambda function, which then kicks off a CI job against your newly created Elastic Beanstalk environment.

Reference:
https://aws.amazon.com/blogs/compute/event-driven-computing-with-amazon-sns-compute-storage-database-and-networking-services/

333. **Correct Answer:** *B*

Reference:
https://d1.awsstatic.com/whitepapers/aws-whitepaper-business-value-of-aws.pdf

334. **Correct Answer:** *C*

Reference:
https://docs.aws.amazon.com/AmazonS3/latest/dev/replication.html

335. **Correct Answer:** *D*

Reference:
https://aws.amazon.com/compliance/shared-responsibility-model/

336. **Correct Answer:** *C*

Reference:
https://aws.amazon.com/devops/partner-solutions/

337. **Correct Answer:** *AD*

Reference:
https://docs.aws.amazon.com/AmazonCloudWatch/latest/monitoring/monitor_estimated_charges_with_cloudwatch.html

338. **Correct Answer:** *B*

Reference:
https://docs.aws.amazon.com/Route53/latest/DeveloperGuide/Welcome.html

339. **Correct Answer:** *C*

Reference: https://aws.amazon.com/guardduty/

340. **Correct Answer:** *A*

Reference:
https://aws.amazon.com/about-aws/whats-new/2019/09/aws-marketplace-easier-to-find-solutions-from-aws-console/

341. **Correct Answer:** *B*

Reference: https://aws.amazon.com/dynamodb/

342. **Correct Answer:** *C*

Reference:

https://docs.aws.amazon.com/AmazonCloudWatch/latest/monitoring/monitor_estimated_charges_with_cloudwatch.html

343. **Correct Answer:** *C*

Reference:

https://aws.amazon.com/getting-started/tutorials/deploy-docker-containers/

344. **Correct Answer:** *A*

Reference:

https://aws.amazon.com/getting-started/tutorials/deliver-content-faster/

345. **Correct Answer:** *AD*

Reference:

https://docs.aws.amazon.com/IAM/latest/UserGuide/best-practices.html

346. **Correct Answer:** *B*

Reference:

https://docs.aws.amazon.com/vpc/latest/userguide/flow-logs.html

347. **Correct Answer:** *C*

AWS Global Accelerator uses the AWS global network to optimize the path from your users to your applications, improving the performance of your trafic by as much as 60%. AWS Global Accelerator continually monitors the health of your application endpoints and redirects trafic to healthy endpoints in less than 30 seconds.

Reference:
https://aws.amazon.com/global-accelerator/?blogs-global-accelerator.sort-by=item.additionalFields.createdDate& blogs-global-accelerator.sort- order=desc&aws-global-accelerator-wn.sort-by=item.additionalFields.postDate Time&aws-global-accelerator-wn.sort-order=desc

348. **Correct Answer:** *AC*

349. **Correct Answer:** *A*

    Reference:
    https://aws.amazon.com/blogs/mt/monitor-and-notify-on-aws-account-root-user-activity/

350. **Correct Answer:** *C*

    Reference:
    https://www.botmetric.com/blog/aws-cloud-architecture-design-principles/

351. **Correct Answer:** *AD*

    Reference: https://aws.amazon.com/snowball/

352. **Correct Answer:** *C*

353. **Correct Answer:** *B*

    Reference:
    https://docs.aws.amazon.com/organizations/latest/userguide/orgs_manage_accounts.html

354. **Correct Answer:** *B*

355. **Correct Answer:** *B*

Reference: https://aws.amazon.com/autoscaling/

356. **Correct Answer:** *C*

Reference:
https://d1.awsstatic.com/whitepapers/aws-security-whitepaper.pdf (36)

357. **Correct Answer:** *C*

Reference:
https://docs.aws.amazon.com/awsaccountbilling/latest/aboutv2/ce-forecast.html

358. **Correct Answer:** *B*

Amazon CloudFront employs a global network of edge locations and regional edge caches that cache copies of your content close to your viewers. Amazon CloudFront ensures that end-user requests are served by the closest edge location. As a result, viewer requests travel a short distance, improving performance for your viewers. For files not cached at the edge locations and the regional edge caches, Amazon CloudFront keeps persistent connections with your origin servers so that those files can be fetched from the origin servers as quickly as possible.

Reference: https://aws.amazon.com/cloudfront/faqs/

359. **Correct Answer:** *B*

Reference:
https://aws.amazon.com/about-aws/global-infrastructure/

360. **Correct Answer:** *A*

Reference: https://aws.amazon.com/ec2/faqs/

361. **Correct Answer:** *B*

Reference:
https://docs.aws.amazon.com/elasticloadbalancing/latest/userguide/what-is-load-balancing.html

362. **Correct Answer:** *CE*

Reference:
https://cloudacademy.com/blog/aws-shared-responsibility-model-security/

363. **Correct Answer:** *B*

Reference:
https://d1.awsstatic.com/whitepapers/AWS_Cloud_Best_Practices.pdf (20)

364. **Correct Answer:** *AE*

Reference:
https://aws.amazon.com/waf/ https://docs.aws.amazon.com/vpc/latest/userguide/vpc-network-acls.html

365. **Correct Answer:** *B*

Reference: https://aws.amazon.com/efs/

366. **Correct Answer:** *BC*

367. **Correct Answer:** *D*

Reference:
https://aimconsulting.com/insights/blog/the-elastic-cloud-opportunity/

368. **Correct Answer:** C

Reference:
https://read.acloud.guru/there-are-four-reasons-to-explain-how-using-aws-can-change-the-economic-model-of-the-it-services-850dcc8ea1aa? gi=3bcf6cd0e1e2

369. **Correct Answer:** A

Reference:
https://docs.aws.amazon.com/AmazonS3/latest/dev/access-control-block-public-access.html

370. **Correct Answer:** A

371. **Correct Answer:** B

Reference:
https://aws.amazon.com/blogs/aws/estimate-your-c/

372. **Correct Answer:** A

Reference:
https://aws.amazon.com/compliance/shared-responsibility-model/

373. **Correct Answer:** AB

Reference: https://aws.amazon.com/autoscaling/faqs/

374. **Correct Answer:** BD

Reference:
https://aws.amazon.com/global-accelerator/faqs/

375. **Correct Answer:** *D*

Reference:

https://aws.amazon.com/premiumsupport/knowledge-center/reactivate-suspended-account/

376. **Correct Answer:** *B*

In a traditional computing environment, you provision capacity based on an estimate of a theoretical maximum peak. This can result in periods where expensive resources are sitting idle or occasions of insuficient capacity. With cloud computing, you can access as much or as little capacity as you need and dynamically scale to meet actual demand, while only paying for what you use.

377. **Correct Answer:** *A*

Reference:

https://www.cloudmanagementinsider.com/ways-to-optimize-aws-cost/

378. **Correct Answer:** *C*

Reference:

https://aws.amazon.com/compliance/shared-responsibility-model/

379. **Correct Answer:** *BC*

380. **Correct Answer:** *B*

Reference:

https://aws.amazon.com/compliance/shared-responsibility-model/

381. **Correct Answer:** *C*

Reference:

https://docs.aws.amazon.com/IAM/latest/UserGuide/
console_controlling-access.html

https://aws.amazon.com/iam/

382. **Correct Answer:** *B*

Reference:

https://aws.amazon.com/artifact/#:~:text=AWS%20Artifact
%20is%20your%20go,reports%20and%20select%20
online%20agreements.

383. **Correct Answer:** *A*

Reference:

https://aws.amazon.com/polly/#:~:text=Amazon%20Polly%
20is%20a%20service,synthesize%20natural%20sounding
%20human%20speech.

384. **Correct Answer:** *B*

385. **Correct Answer:** *C*

Reference:

https://aws.amazon.com/premiumsupport/technology/
trusted-advisor/best-practice-checklist/#Security

386. **Correct Answer:** *A*

Reference:

https://aws.amazon.com/ec2/dedicated-hosts/pricing/

387. **Correct Answer:** *C*

When your web traffic is geo-dispersed, it›s not always feasible and certainly not cost effective to replicate your entire infrastructure across the globe. A CDN provides you the ability to utilize its global network of edge locations to deliver a cached copy of web content such as videos, webpages, images and so on to your customers. To reduce response time, the CDN utilizes the nearest edge location to the customer or originating request location in order to reduce the response time. Throughput is dramatically increased given that the web assets are delivered from cache. For dynamic data, many CDNs can be configured to retrieve data from the origin servers.

Reference:
https://aws.amazon.com/caching/

388. **Correct Answer:** *A*

Reference:
https://d1.awsstatic.com/whitepapers/architecture/AWS_Well-Architected_Framework.pdf (12)

389. **Correct Answer:** *B*

Reference:
https://docs.aws.amazon.com/amazondynamodb/latest/developerguide/SQLtoNoSQL.html

390. **Correct Answer:** *B*

Reference:
https://www.botmetric.com/blog/having-a-disaster-recovery-plan-is-pivotal-the-dos-and-donts-on-aws-cloud/

391. **Correct Answer:** *DE*

Reference: https://aws.amazon.com/organizations/

392. **Correct Answer:** *B*

Reference: https://aws.amazon.com/opsworks/

393. **Correct Answer:** *B*

Reference:
https://docs.aws.amazon.com/awsaccountbilling/latest/
aboutv2/consolidated-billing.html

394. **Correct Answer:** *B*

Reference:
https://aws.amazon.com/tco-calculator/

395. **Correct Answer:** *BD*

Reference: https://aws.amazon.com/directconnect/faqs/

396. **Correct Answer:** *AC*

Reference:
https://aws.amazon.com/compliance/shared-responsibility-
model/

397. **Correct Answer:** *C*

Reference: https://aws.amazon.com/premiumsupport/plans/

398. **Correct Answer:** *D*

Reference: https://aws.amazon.com/rds/faqs/

399. **Correct Answer:** *D*

Reference:
https://jayendrapatil.com/aws-high-availability-fault-tolerance-architecture-certification/

400. **Correct Answer:** *B*

Reference: https://aws.amazon.com/transit-gateway/

Printed in Great Britain
by Amazon

75721868R00119